Praise

'Whether you are raising money, selling a product, managing a crisis, or communicating a political agenda, *The BRILLIANT Communicator* is a must read.'
— **Fadi Ghandour**, Executive Chairman, Wamda Group

'This book is your guide to mastering the art of conveying ideas with impact, ensuring you're not just heard, but sought after. Prepare to rise above the noise and become the obvious choice in your field.'
— **Lady Eve Laws**, serial entrepreneur

'This treasure of a book gives you everything you need to know to catapult your message right inside the heads of those you want to reach. Nima truly inspires you as she takes you on a step-by-step journey to learn how to be The BRILLIANT Communicator.'
— **HRH Princess Rym Ali**, Founder, Jordan Media Institute; President, Amman International Film Festival; President, Anna Lindh Foundation

'Want to take your career and business goals to the next level? Read this book. It helps you dig deeper to get the best out of yourself as a communicator.'
— **Ashraf Shakah**, President, Public Relations and Influence, Memac Ogilvy MENA

THE BRILLIANT COMMUNICATOR

High-impact communication tactics to attract
more clients and amplify your authority

Nima Abu Wardeh

Award-winning BBC broadcaster

Rᵉthink

To the unheard of the world.

For those without a voice.

Contents

Foreword

I have known Nima for years as both a journalist and as someone deeply committed to the issues she covers. She interviewed me several times during her time at the BBC, while I was CEO of Aramex, and from her incisive questions, I learned I needed to be prepared and ready to tell my story, just as she was always prepared to get hers out. In other words, we both wished to achieve a certain communication goal from each interview.

I have found Nima to be a professional communicator who does her homework, knows her subject, studies her interviewees and gets what she wants from every interview and report. As an avid follower of her *Middle East Business Report* on the BBC, I heard from her interesting stories about the region, brilliantly told to keep her audience watching every week when the programme aired.

Communicating brilliantly isn't easy, but there is a method and a process to it. It can be learned and taught, and it can be mastered. Anyone who wants to communicate brilliantly to get the results he or she is hoping for – or, as Nima puts it, get a yes – will benefit tremendously from the content of this excellent book.

Whether you are a CEO of a company, a head of a country, a business development executive, a team leader, a social entrepreneur, a founder of a startup; whether you are raising money, selling a product, managing a crisis, sharing a political agenda; without communicating with and understanding your audience brilliantly, you will not be able to succeed in whatever you are aiming for. Everything you achieve in public life comes down to communicating well.

In her book, Nima puts communicating in a BRILLIANT framework for you. Her system is clear, straight to the point, simple to learn, and effective. I have been in business for more than four decades and I can tell you that as a young entrepreneur – building a company with big ambitions but limited resources – I learned just how crucial communication is and how essential it is to master it, both in a business and a personal setting. I and my team have gone from struggling to survive, to competing with giants, to managing crises during wars and civil disturbances, to taking the company public on Nasdaq – becoming the first Arab-based one to do so by attracting investors in the USA. Communication has always been a core competency for me to succeed as a CEO and a leader in my industry.

Communication is essential for understanding our clients, our investors, the people within the business, giving them confidence, trust, acceptance, and full belief that this is the company they want to be associated with. I would always advise my team leaders and managers to talk the walk, and walk the talk, as that is how to move people from wondering what is in store for them to becoming part of the story. When they feel safe and know that they are in the right place, that's when they become our greatest advocates and believers.

I learned my communication skills on the job, which was a tough way to do it. In a way, though, I was lucky as that was during the pre-internet era, so I had time to learn. Today's hyper-connected social-media world has no mercy; it requires us all to be BRILLIANT communicators from day one. We must all make sure we have the right communication skills before jumping into business. Nima's book has the answers.

Nima Abu Wardeh's BRILLIANT framework is a must for anyone who wants to succeed in business in today's world. You don't have to do it the hard way, learning on the job like I did. In this book, you have an essential resource, whether you're just starting your journey or building on what you have already learned. With her BRILLIANT framework, you will nail it and transcend it, or as Nima herself puts it: 'Step into next you and your brilliant future. Morph into a category of one and become the catalyst for change.'

I have enjoyed this book tremendously and learned a lot from it. As a result, I will share it with all the CEOs and founders of the companies I know and invest in. It is an essential read and tool for anyone in business, and for life as well.

Fadi Ghandour
Executive Chairman, Wamda Group

Introduction

**Communication is the currency that builds
all success.**

Who gets the money? The person with the brilliant idea, or the person who is the brilliant communicator? I'm sure you know the answer.

Being brilliant at both sets you apart. It elevates you to a category of one. You become the only choice, not just another option.

Replace the word 'money' with whatever success is to you, and you get the picture: what and how you communicate is key to turning your version of success into reality. I want to make it easier for you to share your expertise and experience in a way that ensures the right people for you lean in, want more, and will act on what you convey. Doing this well changes everything.

Two realisations led me to shift my focus from working exclusively with the C-suite and those who govern us, to working with people brave enough to create their own version of success. One is the outcomes of funding panels I judged and events I chaired, where startup founders and entrepreneurs vied for the lifeblood that is money, and corporate professionals competed for cash for passion projects ranging from saving turtles to employing battered women. Without exception, the money went to the great communicators – people with superb presence who projected what we tend to call 'confidence' (you'll find my take on this word and why I don't like it in Chapter Three). These individuals owned their space and enrolled disciples.

We remember exceptions and the exceptional. In the context of this book, the exceptions are the few times I was told to stop and leave because the guest didn't want to answer the questions I posed. The exceptional are those few individuals I remember out of the thousands I have interacted with. I remember them for specific reasons – like the CEO of a mining company, who was the most captivating, practical, and relevant speaker at a conference I chaired. I still recall the examples she shared, which brought to life what others talked about but hadn't actioned. Standing tall in her scuffed cowboy boots and androgynous grey suit, microphone in hand, she owned that stage – and commanded every bit of our attention.

I also remember the excellent guests we had on speed dial for the television programmes I presented. We did everything in our power not to default to having them on, but boy were they super at simplifying complicated information, stating the 'obvious' (once stated or in hindsight), and putting it into a relatable context. They each represented a safe pair of hands who always delivered – and got extra airtime as a result.

My goal is to enable as many people as I can to be exceptional when sharing their experience and expertise.

The other epiphany I had relates to people who get in touch wanting me to advocate on their behalf. There is one me, and a multitude of worthy causes – the most powerful way I can help is by enabling others to become their own biggest advocates and best spokespeople, so that they are able to shine a light on their important work and how it helps, and achieve the results they seek.

I want this for you too.

This book is the product of decades spent interviewing, training, and working alongside thousands of brilliant minds at the top of their game: leaders, entrepreneurs, and subject matter experts. A big 'aha!' moment for me was recognising that my definition of communication is different to theirs.

Before then, I'd often feel frustrated – for them, with them, and on behalf of the audience at conferences or during interviews I conducted – because there was so much meaningless chat and 'communication' that was frankly boring, irrelevant, and not memorable. I then transitioned to feeling frustrated for the people communicating because they didn't know how to do it well, in a way that would further drive their success. They were 'doing their job' – sharing their agenda, achievements, and latest developments, but were they communicating effectively? It depends on how you define it.

The prevailing approach is to prioritise what the organisation or speaker is doing, without considering or linking it to what matters to the individuals those communicating aim to engage. It's an inherent outcome of being human, as you will discover in Chapter Two. As a result, people go through the motions of communicating, but miss the true purpose: deepening relationships with their ideal target audience and shaping a specific perception of them in that audience's mind.

Whether I'm in the role of journalist, chair, or panel moderator, my desire is to move the conversation forward – the optimal outcome is connecting ideas and information, uncovering why an issue is important, and revealing interesting insights that are relevant to my audience. My role is not to highlight what's important to your target audience or stakeholder. That's your role, and it's critical to your success.

Connecting three elements is essential: what you as a speaker say, what you want your audience to know, and what the audience is interested in hearing more about. This tends to be missing. The disconnect is getting these three elements to line up. Your success hinges on getting the right people to take note and approach you for the next step, which happens at the intersection of this trifecta.

This book integrates, then unifies these elements in a way that streamlines your thinking and process, enabling you to draw in and connect with the person whose attention you want. It sets out how you can implant an idea, an emotion, a desired action in their mind – one that serves them and positions you as their best solution. Think of this book as a guide to using communication as a business strategy, leading your ideal stakeholder to follow your path and act on your ask. Achieving this requires you to shape your message to suit the person, the occasion, and your intended outcome in a specific way.

Having trained hundreds and interviewed thousands, I know that transforming the way you think, write, and speak is key. In the chapters to follow, you will discover why becoming a known brilliant communicator in your field serves and elevates you, and you will recognise the significant opportunity that our current times present. My hope is that you act on it.

If I was to summarise what this book is about, it would be this:

Ways to get the right people to
lean in, tune in, and want in.

Your 'in' changes as your wants and needs change. You might need funding, aim to close more clients or investors, seek approval from a regulator, want a journalist to interview you, or hope to be chosen as a conference speaker. Defining the 'in' influences the 'what' that you communicate. Delivering it in a certain way means that you stand out and are remembered for the right reasons – then comes your transition to power.

Let me give you an example. When chairing or moderating, I wield significant power. I summarise what someone says, whether during a keynote or as part of a panel discussion. I highlight what I believe are the most pertinent, relevant (to the audience and the times we live in), interesting points they've shared.

My interpretation dominates and is planted in people's minds if the person speaking doesn't have a handle on how to communicate brilliantly. However, if a speaker does a great job of conveying the information that they want to stick, they dictate the embedded highlights. The same applies to media interviews, pitching, and, in short, every interaction.

Here's my message to you. If there is something important you want to get across, do it in a way that leaves no room for misunderstanding or missed opportunity. Make your take the prevailing one. If you don't, someone else will – with their agenda and interpretation at the core.

What to expect from this book

This is a book of three parts: Build, Share, Elevate. Every part consists of three chapters that combine to form what you will come to know as The BRILLIANT Framework. If you would like to document your thinking and complete the exercises outlined in this book, you can download and print the accompanying BRILLIANT Communicator Workbook at: www.thebrilliantcommunicator.com/book-resources.

What is The BRILLIANT Framework? It is your practical reality-based guide to communicating with impact and influence, enabling you to be heard and chosen in a world overwhelmed with too much information and increasing numbers of people banging their own drum.

I wish many of the thousands of people I have interacted with – on stage at conferences, in media set-
tings, at internal town halls and events – had had this
guide. It would have made for less time wasted and
better outcomes, because they would have piqued
the interest of the right stakeholders, attracted more
opportunity, and had much more engaging, credible
interactions.

Communicating with impact and influence is a core
skill. There's nothing soft about it.

Here's to cutting through the noise, rising above the
din, and being sought out for your unique approach
to what you are brilliant at. Here's to you elevating
your influence and being the obvious choice. Here's
to you becoming The BRILLIANT Communicator in
your field.

PART ONE
BUILD

S econd to breathing, communication is what we do
most in life.

Communication transcends the spoken word. It's
what you put out – broadcast with words, body,
behaviour. It's content you create to disseminate. And
it's the dialogue you hold within. Like breathing, it's
essential, facilitating your outward expressions and
your internal musings.

In Build, you'll embark on a journey of self-reflection
and discovery – revealing what being a brilliant communicator does for you, your life, and the lives of
those you care about. This part also sets the scene so
that you know what you're up against and how you
are an asset. We'll start with how the elements of the

THE BRILLIANT COMMUNICATOR

book come together to create a pathway for you to walk along, and why taking ownership of your expertise, experience, knowledge, and insight is critical.

We will establish 'chase' – what are you chasing? – and define what you are choosing. Clarity around this fuels your path. Make it powerful enough and it'll keep you dedicated to becoming The BRILLIANT Communicator in your field.

Part One also shares why now is the time to become the best communicator you can possibly be, and how communicating effectively with yourself sets the stage for success with others. Each element follows on from the previous one and sets a solid base for the next step.

Let us begin.

ONE

B – Begin and Believe

BELIEVE	**R**EFLECT	**I**NSPIRE
LISTEN	**L**EVEL UP	**I**NVESTIGATE
AHA!	**N**AIL IT	**T**RANSCEND

What opportunity did you miss out on recently? It could be signing a client, pitching for a contract, or putting yourself forward for a media interview or to speak at an event. If you did participate, perhaps you missed out because you didn't get the outcome you desired.

Why do you think this happened? More importantly, would you rather miss out on the next opportunity or master it?

Communication is a fickle thing. There are umpteen ways to do it and formats to utilise. How do you know which one will enable you to excel at it?

In this chapter, you'll discover the ingredients of The BRILLIANT Communicator, the framework you can implement to become one, and how the elements of this book fit together to form The BRILLIANT Communicator Opportunity Matrix. By the end, you will be firmly rooted in the realisation that being *you* is an advantage, and that becoming The BRILLIANT Communicator in your field unlocks your next opportunity. The better you get at it, the 'luckier' you'll become.

The BRILLIANT Framework: Crafting your strategy

BRILLIANT is the name, the aim, and the method. Over the next few chapters, I will guide you through the elements of the framework, each representing a distinct approach that I encourage you to adopt. Implementing these principles develops your personal strategy for achieving communication success, and thereby your version of success. Note that I use the word 'stakeholder' to refer to the person you want to engage with.

Each letter in the B-R-I-L-L-I-A-N-T Framework represents a principle to be mastered:

- **B – Begin and Believe.** Cultivate a deep belief in the value of what you do and know, and how it enables you to pursue the work you love and build the life you aspire to. Pinpoint the reason this version of success is important to you. Make it compelling and you'll stay the course.

- **R – Reflect, Reframe, and Refine.** Reflect on your wants and needs, reframe your challenges, and refine what you must do to make your aspirations your lived reality.

- **I – Inspire.** Communication is your chance to inspire and motivate. Harness the power of emotional connection to elevate your communication from informative to transformative.

- **L – Listen.** Tune in to what your stakeholder says, feels, dreams of. Including these elements in what you share signals you understand them deeply. They will then listen.

- **L – Level up.** Enhance your impact, zone in on your unique take and magic, and prepare for the worst. Discover what's needed to get to your next level.

- **I – Investigate to Iterate.** Explore your credibility footprint, experiment with new ways of adding to it. Stay adaptable, try out new formats, embrace feedback, tweak and repeat.

- **A – Aha!** Astonish with insight, be obsessive about your stakeholder, own your agenda, deliver on purpose.

- **N – Nail it.** Bring the elements together. Ensure your message is not just heard, but felt, driving home the core of what you wish to achieve with clarity and brilliance.

- **T – Transcend.** Step into 'next you' and your brilliant future. Create a category of one and become the catalyst for change.

To bring these elements to pass, you need to take on the role of CEO.

CEO of Credible You

Being The BRILLIANT Communicator isn't only about communication. It necessitates taking deliberate ownership of your knowledge, experience, and expertise – I call this becoming the CEO of Credible You. This is made up of two components: credibility and ownership.

You want to be known for the right thing by the right people. Without being credible and brilliant at what you know and do, you have nothing to build on. Without taking ownership of your credibility and brilliance, you will not become The BRILLIANT Communicator.

People tend to dismiss what they know, considering it obvious or not important. This is misguided and means they miss out – we'll discuss this more in Chapter Six. Here is a mindset that helps: embrace and celebrate what you know right now. Recognise your value, what you offer, and how you can help. If you don't believe in and embrace your worth, others won't either. The decision and deep conviction that what you know right now is all you need is critical to becoming The BRILLIANT Communicator.

Taking ownership of how you communicate with your stakeholders is also critical to being the CEO of Credible You. Let's set the groundwork.

Communication never happens in isolation. It happens when you transfer an idea from your head and plant it in someone else's. You do this when you are in a meeting, speaking one to one, pitching, on stage, in the media, on a podcast, using LinkedIn, and so on. Think of it as transmitting, receiving and having the significance of your idea realised. For example, if you record a video or write a post, communication only occurs when you put it out, it is received by someone, and they grasp its relevance – potentially responding or taking action as a result.

For the purpose of this book, I will lean into verbal communication when considering examples, because it brings together all the elements needed for any type of communication, including choosing words, how you sound, and how you are when doing this. You can go on to use these components together or independently, depending on what medium you will employ to communicate. Plus, viewing interactions through this lens frames them with the ultimate goal in mind. Here's what I mean.

Verbal communication is a joint activity. When two brains communicate well, they synchronise and couple with each other – think of it as dancing in parallel.[1] The greater the understanding, and the more the stakeholder 'gets' what the speaker is saying, the greater the coupling.

To increase the probability of this happening – in the context of becoming The BRILLIANT Communicator in your field – you must nail your 3Ws:

- What you want to be known for

- Who by

- Why they should consider you as their solution

Without answering the 3Ws, you're wasting time and energy. What you craft transpires as missed opportunity rather than a solid business strategy. Combining Credible You with your ability to communicate effectively is how you become The BRILLIANT Communicator.

Communicating effectively sounds so bland, so boring. It's anything but. It's knowing what to say and how to say it in a way that interests the stakeholder you want or need buy-in from. It's how you become known for the right thing by the right people and move closer to your big 'I made it!' – your success, however you define it.

The BRILLIANT Communicator's Opportunity Matrix: Mapping your path

What yes is going to change your world? What result do you want from the person you're engaging with that will change your life, your day, your mood?

'Yes' is your ultimate goal every time you interact; it's the one thing you're after whenever you communicate. Getting it starts with being very clear about the specific yes you want.

Is it yes for money? Perhaps you need funding, a sale, to seal a contract. Is it recognition that you're after? It could be a position you're looking to secure, an invitation to speak at an event where you hope to raise your profile, or an accolade you wish to win.

> You're only one yes away from changing your life.

To increase the chance of the yes happening, provide the stakeholder who has the power to grant it with a clear path to the specific action you want them to take, and make it compelling enough for them to follow through. Do this right, and people buy into you, your vision, your process.

Success isn't only about achieving your big 'I made it!', though. It's about sustaining it too – being able to show up and keep showing up. For this to happen, every aspect of you and your life needs to be OK. Where are you great at getting across what you want, what you need, what you do? Where do you struggle? Are you focusing on your professional success and perhaps neglecting your personal fulfilment?

I'm reminded of a time I was in Davos for the World Economic Forum's annual shindig – where the 'great and good' gather to debate and deliberate over the state of the world and their industries, as well as dine, dance, and broker deals. One of the sessions was 'How to be a better husband'. True success lies in both your professional and personal life being sustainable.

There are only three things you communicate: what you want, what you need, and what you do. The powerful men in Davos were super at doing this in their professional lives, but recognised they could do better in their personal domains. Becoming The BRILLIANT Communicator enables you to thrive in all aspects of life.

Getting buy-in from the right people entails changing the way you think, write, and speak. When I train people,

I explain that they have all the information and knowledge they need to do this, it's a case of reorganising and reprioritising it in their mind. The same is true for you.

Want, need, do. Think, write, speak. I will be using these words as anchors throughout the book – asking you to reflect on, consider, and drill down to what it is you want and need to create and sustain your version of success, and what you must do so that what you want and need become your lived reality. Together, these words form The BRILLIANT Communicator Opportunity Matrix.

Integrating The BRILLIANT Framework into the matrix maps out your path to elevating your influence and making you the obvious choice in your field. You transform from being an option to becoming the solution, from chasing opportunity to being chosen for it.

	WANT	NEED	DO
T H I N K	**B** BELIEVE	**R** REFLECT	**I** INSPIRE
W R I T E	**L** LISTEN	**L** LEVEL UP	**I** INVESTIGATE
S P E A K	**A** AHA!	**N** NAIL IT	**T** TRANSCEND

This is how the book fits together. Each of the three parts – '*Build*', '*Share*', '*Elevate*' – segments into three chapters. All together, these nine chapters spell out The BRILLIANT Framework. The words want, need, and do are anchors throughout, while think, write, speak sum up every chapter.

The more proficient you become at processing information in the BRILLIANT way, the more efficient you will be at applying it when interacting, and the higher the probability of getting your yes.

Crises

Have you noticed that, for all the information out there, there's rarely an answer to your query? You could experience this when researching a topic for a presentation or looking up the best kit to buy for your (insert hobby).

We're bombarded with more material than we can properly process and manage, making it increasingly challenging to find what we need. This is the crisis of being overwhelmed and under informed.

The issue is compounded by another crisis: experts aiming to enlighten and establish their authority being misled by myth and misinformation. Their content falls flat, not due to a lack of knowledge, but because they focus on the wrong things when they communicate, misguided by flawed teachings, providing content that misses their purpose and ultimately adding to the vast expanse of data that doesn't enlighten.

A prime example is the widespread misinterpretation of the 7:38:55 rule from Professor Albert Mehrabian's 1967 research, where many communication experts wrongly instruct that only 7% of communication impact comes from words, with 38% from tonality and 55% from body language.[2]

Mehrabian's flawed experiment was focused on the context of a speaker sharing their feelings and attitudes. He wanted to discover how believable a speaker is to listeners when their words and nonverbal cues don't align. For instance, saying 'I am sorry' with a smirk would lead to the dismissal of the words in favour of the body language.

The result is that many alleged experts extol that 93% of communication is non-verbal.

My take? Words matter more than you might think. Get them right and you can focus on refining other aspects of how you communicate. Get them wrong and your message goes unheard. Chapter Four takes you through how to excel at picking the right words to suit the occasion.

Don't let the crisis of missing out due to misinformation get you, and don't let how you communicate undermine you. Here's what I mean.

This week, I – sort of – watched a founder I admire being interviewed. It was a snippet uploaded to LinkedIn that was just under three minutes long – I made myself watch twenty seconds. Why? She said many words, but her thoughts were not connected. It was too much effort trying to stick with it, so I switched away, and this is someone I am rooting for. I wonder how many others did the same.

You've done the hard work of becoming an expert or starting a business. Don't let the crisis of clarity and myth reduce your visibility and recognition. It holds you back. As can the crisis of drinking your own Kool-Aid. You'll find out more in Chapter Five.

Why bother?

There's a direct line linking how well you communicate with how well your life turns out. Being a BRILLIANT communicator means visibility and recognition. Being known and recognised for what you offer is your path to success. Converting interest into action means achieving the outcome you desire.

'I do any job well apart from presenting it.' This was shared with me by someone who founded a software as a service (SaaS) business while working full-time in a high-profile corporate job. Their plan was to leave the job and work on the startup once they had money in the bank to fund it.

Here's the rest of what they said:

> 'If I could communicate with ease, I would be
> able to present better, which would probably
> result in more investments, more partnerships.
> Just getting the visibility out there. Visibility
> both internally and among clients. I've gotten
> a few opportunities with public speaking,
> and I chickened out of most of the major ones.
> I do my job well. I do any job well, apart from
> presenting it. Yes, effective communication
> gets recognition.'

Without knowing anything else about the person who said this or what their situation is, you can appreciate the impact that being able to present, speak at events, be interviewed by the media, and pitch will have on the business they're building and the life of the founder.

What about you? How would your life be if you were a better communicator?

While you mull that over, know that billionaire Warren Buffett declared that his number-one investment has been learning how to communicate well.[3] He says that all the brain power in the world won't matter without this one key skill. I agree.

Communication is currency.

Summary

In its simplest form, communication boils down to getting something from your head into someone else's. How well you do this determines the chance of getting your yes and moving one step closer to the outcome that you desire.

Having gone through the Begin element of BRILLIANT in Chapter One, you can see how we are all drowning in information, but have no answers, and that myth and misinformation around how to communicate well mean you miss out. You can also see how communication becomes more manageable and less intimidating when you break it down to three elements: what you want, what you need, and what you do. To do this well, you must transform the way you think, write, and speak.

The B of BRILLIANT also stands for Believe. It's about believing in yourself, your life, your vision of the future, your version of success – elements we dive into in Chapter Two. It's also about believing and trusting in the process I am guiding you through, so that you become the obvious choice in your field and transition from chasing opportunity to being chosen for it.

Do you believe? I hope so.

Think. Reflect on how effective communication could have changed the outcome of a recent missed opportunity.

Write. Define the specific yes you're seeking, identify who it needs to come from, and consider what motivates them to grant it to you.

Speak. Do yourself justice when you communicate and become known and recognised for what you do and offer.

TWO

R – Reflect, Reframe, and Refine

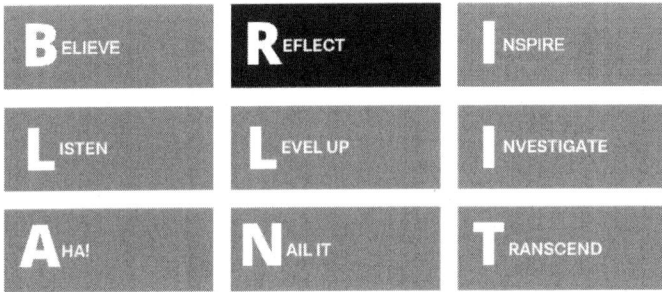

BELIEVE	**R**EFLECT	**I**NSPIRE
LISTEN	**L**EVEL UP	**I**NVESTIGATE
AHA!	**N**AIL IT	**T**RANSCEND

S omething isn't quite the way you want it to be. Do you know what it is? Do you know how to change it? And do you know who holds the key to making the change you need?

Status quo is the problem.

Status quo can be a killer. If not of dreams, then often of passion.

In this chapter, you'll reflect on what you want or need to change in your life, reframe what's holding you back, and refine how you move forward to achieve your desired outcome. This involves tuning into yourself, uncovering your current objectives, and unveiling your core message. It includes reframing interactions as an opportunity to be your best spokesperson and advocate, and refining your approach to being known for your expertise.

Simply put, let's define what success looks like for you, and why investing in effective communication is the shortest, surest path to it.

Want, need, do – digging deeper

Want. What do you want for yourself? This is the fun part! It's where you get to dream, wish, uncover your version of success and what your best life looks like. This is why the symbol for want is a heart – it's what your heart desires. It could be building a mega business, working part time, being location agnostic, or becoming a known expert delivering high-level talks in person.

Dare to define what you want. Include how you want to live, how you want to work, and how you want to show up for yourself and for those you care about. Your want generates a set of things that need to happen for you to succeed.

Need. What do you need? This relates to your unique circumstance and life, along with what you want to create for yourself.

Pinpoint the specific things that you need to be and do, the exact things that must happen for your want to become reality. Examples include skills or experience to acquire, funding that must materialise, teams to be curated, licences to obtain, and building a fandom of people eager for more from you – those who will buy into you and your offer.

Do. Define what you must do to obtain what you need. This includes being known for your expertise, product, method. It involves expanding your authority, credibility, and influence, and becoming the go-to person for what you want to do more of – all of which feeds into realising your want. Examples include write a book, be interviewed by the media, guest on podcasts, speak at key events, and have online assets that showcase your expertise and brilliance. More on this in Part Two.

Unveiling your life's desires solidifies your 'Why should I do this?' Make it inspiring enough for you to commit to, then meticulously evaluate your ambitious wants, fundamental needs, and the actionable steps required to bridge the gap between your current reality and your aspiration. Don't stagnate in your status quo.

It's not your fault

Can you communicate? Of course you can... to an extent.

There's a gap. I call it the communication conundrum. We're taught the alphabet, we know how to structure sentences, read, write, and speak, and we assume that's enough to communicate, but it isn't if the purpose is to get specific people to pay attention, agree to an ask, take action. Speaking doesn't mean you're being listened to. Writing doesn't mean you will be read. Someone reading your work doesn't mean they take it in. You can do all this, and neither communicate nor be recognised as the expert you are.

People who are great at the intangible ability to communicate with impact and influence are the ones who do exceptionally well in life and business, even if what they're selling is rubbish. They capture people's attention and their money.

Most people don't achieve greatness because they prioritise their own interests and agenda.[4] I invite you to reframe your thinking: focus on others to benefit yourself. As you read on, you'll discover how.

I recently endured a call with a provider I was interested in hiring. They didn't ask what my specific need or want is, and spent half an hour pitching what they do, and can do. It was all about them, nothing about me. I got off the call as quickly as I could. I see this 'all about me' or 'talk at not with people' approach on stage and when interviewing for the media a lot.

The focus on self can surface due to other factors too. Here's an example of what I mean. I asked a client – a company's top executive – what three things she wanted to be known for. Her immediate response was that she is the best person for the job – she was newly appointed – and that she never makes mistakes. I forget the third point, because it was more of the same. These answers come from a defensive place. She was telling, proving, batting away the naysayers.

Imagine if she had said something like, 'I am the go-to expert for X, different to the competition because of Y, and I bring Z to this role.'

'Proving' is a person justifying something. It's their pain at the core, which is draining and a turn-off for stakeholders.

Sharing what you know to be true and being your credible expert self is very different. It's energising and attractive. It involves stepping away from answering the question with your self at the centre, and supplanting it with how you best serve a client – the X in the example above.

Think of it as the difference between being an answer-person and your own spokesperson. An answer-person answers the question – often with a tell or prove – and misses the opportunity to establish their credibility in an elevated way. A spokesperson takes a metaphorical step back, understands how the question provides the chance to share the key idea they want to embed in their ideal stakeholder's mind. It's a tactical approach that *ahem* proves they are the best option, because they are.

The person I was training secured a coveted and much-chased government contract two weeks after our session with her new frame of mind in place. Your next step happens with the right people when you are your expert credible self and your best spokesperson. It won't happen if you get stuck overthinking – which is what we'll tackle next.

Stop cerebralising

Cerebralising is a term I coined for the tendency to overthink and analyse to the point of becoming trapped in your brain. This mental gridlock stops you from taking the necessary steps to assert 'This is my knowledge, and I want to be recognised for it.'

Cerebralising killed the communicator.

Getting comfortable with what you will share is a foundational step to overcoming the impasse of cerebralising. To do this, kick-start your cognitive engine: process your big ideas, your way, your take on things. Connecting dots and information happens more fluidly when you know how you process thoughts best – are you a speaker, a writer, a doodler? What helps you reveal your thinking and see or recognise how your knowledge, experience, and way of sharing fit together?

I use coloured sticky notes and whiteboards to create word collages when structuring something like a video series, an online programme, this book. It enables me to get my fix of visuals, colour, contrast, and capturing an idea in a word or three. Plus it's easy to change the flow and what's connected to what as my thinking evolves.

I also think and process information by writing and speaking, then fermenting – or at least marinating (less time) – the info in my mind. I have tomes of hand-written notes and a tonne of voice recordings that I don't give a second glance or listen to. They do their job by stirring up all manner of things – links, realisations, ways of putting what I know to be true, all whirring away in the background as I go through the day (and night).

Many of the clever people I work with struggle if they sit to type – because they lock into cerebralising mode. Most unlock their cognitive engine by creating voice-notes, then transcribing and refining them. Do this away from your workstation to maximise whirr. Go for a walk, ride a bike – be in motion. Your sub-conscious kicks in – mulling over points and realising additional things as you go about your business. Mundane tasks also free the brain to have 'Aha!' moments (taking a shower or emptying the dish-washer are prime examples).[5]

Writing an unedited thought dump is another fabu-lous way of doing this. Put pen to paper.[6] Don't type. Writing by hand uses more neurones and creates more connections in your brain.[7]

How do you think best? For me, vocalising my knowl-edge while walking is my number-one aid. It is lib-erating. It frees my thoughts and gets them flowing. Clarifying. It crystallises my thinking. Plus it sharp-ens and refines my message, boosting its impact.

You find your voice by using it. You create your narra-tive by expressing it. This is how you break free from cerebralising.

Forget storytelling

How many times have you heard that you must tell a story? You can tell all the stories in the world, but if you don't provide a reason for people to pay attention to what you're putting out, you've lost.

The story isn't the point, but if you're not careful, it can become your focus – to the detriment of your interaction. When people are told to use a story to communicate best, it's often interpreted as needing to structure a tale with a beginning, middle, and end, complete with characters, conflicts, resolutions, or lessons. Whether it's a work of fiction or a personal anecdote, it's tough to have a fantastic story, be a great storyteller, and make it relevant to your audience or stakeholder.

Clients of mine have signed multiple seven-figure contracts with no story – because they excelled at being the voice inside their client's head, capturing their interest and eagerness to experience the outcome described. This has happened in both private meetings and as a result of speaking on stage.

It's not about the story. A story is a vehicle for getting information across. The purpose of most presentations or pitches is to pass on information, to start dialogue, to bring about decisions, to prompt specific action as a result.

Successful communication is not about fixating on telling stories.

It is not, folks, it is not. Approach interactions with purpose. Define the yes you want, and who you want it from. Tailor the content to that. Give examples that showcase your expertise – the realities that you deliver, the change you facilitate, the transformation your client goes through. These become your stories.

Am I saying stories are not fabulous vehicles? Not at all. In my role as a journalist and writer, of course I tell stories. Often, I explain a significant issue by telling a story through the lens of someone's experience, so you might think I am contradicting myself by telling you to 'forget storytelling'. A more accurate heading would be 'forget focusing on storytelling – for now'. The pressure of needing to tell a story can send some into a stress spiral. Reframing what a story is and how you can reveal yours is the point. As you evolve, your interactions can become next level by incorporating metaphors and other storytelling techniques. But first, establish the foundation of how to think about and deliver on what you want to achieve.

Every interaction has a purpose. What's yours? What examples bring it to life? Figure this out and fixate on it, then the stories tell themselves.

The opportunity

Be the guiding light. Provide answers. Share your insight. Become the solution. It's the most powerful thing you can do.

None of this happens if you are the world's best-kept secret. Brilliant, but not known by the right people for the right thing.

If you want people with the power to change your life – people who will hire you, invest in you, or buy from you – to stick around, pay attention, and take the next step with you, you must excel at showcasing and sharing your solution, method, expertise in a way that serves them. You owe it to yourself and to those you care about.

If you are responsible for people's livelihoods, running an organisation, or creating a product that changes people's lives, it's your duty to master communicating what you do, how it helps, and why it's important. You do this best by becoming the trusted resource and shining a light on your superior solution. It is your chance to drive meaningful change and make a significant impact on the causes and communities that matter to you. This is the perfect time to do this because of the advent of artificial intelligence (AI) – not only due to the volume of information that doesn't inform being churned out, but crucially because there's only so much human-hacking an algorithm can do.

At the time of writing this, I am looking for a production outfit that leans into human power, and was thrilled when told: 'No, we don't use AI, and we don't outsource.' AI doesn't do what I call spider-web thinking, where you see a headline, hear snippets of an interesting conversation in the supermarket, or have an 'Aha!' moment during a conference coffee break. Thoughts that arise when you're listening to an interview or see a sign when on a walk. All of these combine to form connections or insights that lead to a revelation, because you've knitted data points together in a way only you – a human, and you specifically – can weave from your lived reality and experiences – everything that's gone into your life so far.

The advent of AI has put a premium on being human. The way we weave and process is profound. Use the tech, don't outsource to it. Instead, have a play and a ponder. Its input gets you tweaking, enabling you to leverage content and information you already have, so you can re-use and re-purpose.

My musician son and his friends use bits of metal, wood, plastic – instruments and objects – to make magic and instil epic emotion. Consider this: the Fender guitar was nothing without Jimi Hendrix. AI is nothing without you. Channel your inner Hendrix.

Become the reliable resource for relevant information. Slice through the overwhelm. Lean into you. The power of 'human' is unmatched. Use it.

Summary

Reflect on what you want out of life and how you can sustain your self and your living. Define what's needed to build your best life – one that doesn't break you, and that you don't need a break from.

The key takeaway from Reflect, Reframe, and Refine is that your success starts with defining what you want, and then shifting focus to the stakeholders with the power to make it happen. What do they want from work and life? Focusing on their want, which you are great at delivering, is how you get yours.

Think. Contemplate what you want from work and life, and what needs to be different for you to stay on the path to your version of success.

Write. Draft your big 'I made it!' – your desired success – and start distilling your brilliance and getting it out of your head.

Speak. Be the trusted source of credible information, provide answers to queries and concerns. Become your stakeholder's salvation and your own spokesperson.

THREE

I – Inspire

BELIEVE	**R**EFLECT	**I**NSPIRE
LISTEN	**L**EVEL UP	**I**NVESTIGATE
AHA!	**N**AIL IT	**T**RANSCEND

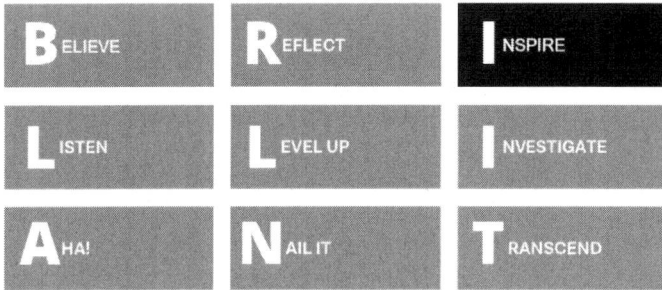

The best communication elicits emotion – people need something that moves them. Inspiration is the most potent feeling to instil because it is to uplift, to show the way, to share that there is a way.

Inspiration is more than an emotion; it's a catalyst, a spark that fuses hope with a resounding 'Yes, we can'. This chapter shares elements that form it.

Here, you discover how you can create emotion – within yourself and others. You will drill down to why success hinges on shifting your focus away from yourself, and you will discover the DNA of The BRILLIANT Communicator. The purpose is to transform words into a compelling force, a magnetic pull that moves people and occasionally mountains, turning possibility into reality.

What emotion do you want to evoke and leave people with? By starting with the end in mind, you deliberately build the emotion into every step.

This chapter is about defining your destination.

Inside out

Your inner emotions influence others; they leak out and people pick up on them. No one will remember your every word or every action. They will remember how they feel around you, and they will decide – subconsciously or occasionally exclaiming out loud – whether they want more of that feeling, and therefore you… or not.

The feeling spills over into decisions they make about you, your product, your ask, the thing that you're sharing, which is why it's important you channel energy that enables you to show up as your best self.

How you are seen starts with how you see yourself.

What if you are nervous or concerned? The great news is that there are simple zero-cost tech-free hacks that you can apply any time, any place, to up your internal chemistry, just like that. Boosting your internal chemistry before you walk into a conference or boardroom, or record yourself on video, changes your external chemistry, which affects how people interact with you, feel around you and respond to you, and the decisions they make as a result.

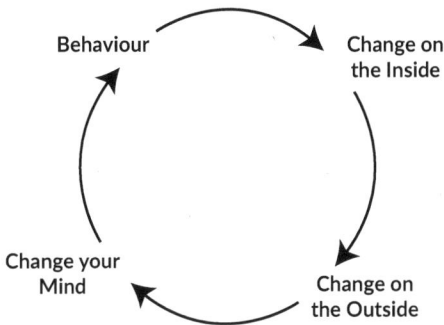

Behaviour — Change on the Inside — Change on the Outside — Change your Mind (cycle diagram)

Research indicates you can achieve this by smiling – even if you don't feel like it.[8] The body can't tell the difference, so it still reacts with the lovely positive brain chemicals that smiling releases – those that make us feel good and reduce stress from head to toe. The opposite is said to be true too, so beware the frown or scowl.[9]

How we use our body affects how we feel, how we see ourselves, and how others see us. Your body speaks all the time. It speaks first and can reveal your subconscious thoughts without you realising it.

I was struck by this when going through professional photos of an event I chaired. In one, my body was screaming 'This is bullshit!' to an answer being given: a snooty facial expression, looking down my nose, head held high, tipped back ever so slightly, very straight back, hands on my lap – trying to physically distance myself as much as possible from the person and what he was extolling. These were micro moves and positions that were not deliberate or intentional – it's only in looking at the photographs that I see them.

In another image, I am leaning in, head tilted slightly, hands embracing the table, engaged and actively listening to what was being shared. The photograph says, 'I like what this person is saying and how they join the dots.'

You give off a vibe all the time. What will it be?

This is not an invitation for you to decipher what people are thinking of you when you speak – you can never control that. The only thing you control is how you show up – and what you share. Focus on what you can do so you don't kick yourself for not having said something or for the way you were when you shared. Do it right, and your stakeholders will all be leaning in for more.

Body-hacks to charge you up include physical actions like jumping jacks or circling your arms. You might be relieved to know that simply taking up more space – what's known as power posing – is also reported to increase the chances of success or getting the yes you want.[10] Research on this has sparked debate, but many find it helps.

The takeaway here is: you won't be able to inspire if you don't feel inspired. Will you use body-hacks to charge yourself up and improve your chance of success?

When your body feels better, you feel better, people around you feel better, and they want more of you, but it's all pointless if you don't share something of value with those whose attention you seek. Here's how.

Stakeholder-centric for win-win

It's not about you. Your wants and needs become reality when you get buy-in from the stakeholder you need on-side. A potential client, your partner in life, your team member – whoever it is you need that yes from, that's your stakeholder.

The stakeholder will change as your priorities and phases evolve. The process remains: you need a yes. The yes gets you a step closer to your 'I made it!'.

Enter the realm of what I call stakeholder-centric communication. It's never about you. It's always about the person you want a yes from. Put them, their wants, their needs first, and you'll get yours. This is the perspective to get ahead.

The biggest mistake people I have interviewed and worked with have made is that their perspective dominates. Their view of the world, their agenda, their ambition is prioritised. It's all me, me, me – I want, need, do. Having conducted over 10,000 interviews, I can safely say this is a human default mode of interacting, regardless of rank or intellect.

Your perspective is vital – define it, acknowledge it, get it out of you and into your planning process. Doing this means you won't be clouded by it. Then park it, and only look through the lens of your stakeholder's perspective while constructing your communication piece. What's important to them? Why should they care about this thing that you want them to say yes to? It's that simple, but we're not trained to think this way.

Understanding and prioritising the wants, needs, and desires of those you seek buy-in from dramatically increases the likelihood of achieving your goals. People are looking for themselves in what you share. Your perspective is key, but your stakeholder's perspective is how you bring about change, which (eventually) makes your perspective and priority a reality. Theirs trumps yours – every time.

Interest, don't inform

You won't have the chance to inspire anyone if they're not interested in what you're sharing – so that's step one. Get them interested.

Imagine this. You're a speaker at a significant industry event, your product is perfect for the audience, you want them to buy from you.

First, you freak out, wondering how you're going to nail the opportunity. Then you figure out a simple way to get everyone in the room raising their hand and engaging. That's what you start with.

Boom! All hands go up. **Kapaw!** The audience gives you a 98% speaker satisfaction rating. $$Kerching!$$ They queue up to take the next step during the coffee break and after the event.

This really happened to a client, Noor Jibril, a healthcare expert at Medtronic:

'While I was presenting, I asked a question, and the entire audience raised their hands, which made me realise they were all interested and that I'd nailed it! I got a satisfaction rate of 98% from the attendees and many people approached me for my expertise. This led to me launching projects in new regions.
'I had the same expertise, capabilities, and passion before this, but I was given an opportunity to present and used Nima's strategy to help me showcase what I can offer in a way that made me more visible, approachable, and heard.'

(Side note: the next best score was 74%, so this wasn't an audience handing out high scores willy-nilly.)

The key to this was Noor starting the talk in a way that would get buy-in from every person there, each one of whom was an ideal client. It involved taking her corporate hat off and looking at the issue through human eyes. The result was the signing of contracts to the tune of many zeros. This is the power of communicating with impact and influence in action.

Did this change in approach to communication and realising opportunity affect what happened next in her career? Of course it did. She went on to be one of only thirty women worldwide chosen as Forbes Ignite Impact Fellows, and her star continues to rise.

> Interest, don't inform. This is now
> your communicating norm.

If time permits, you can then go on to inform. The point is: out with expert and corporate speak, in with human interest. Interesting the person you want a yes from is your primary objective. The rest follows.

The 3Cs

Credible. Comfortable. Consistent. These 3Cs are at the very heart of what defines a brilliant communicator.

Let's examine them:

1. **Credible.** You know your stuff. You are an expert and are brilliant at what you do, right? Therefore, you are credible.

2. **Comfortable.** There will always be something you're uncomfortable doing; the only way to overcome this is to acquire the skills and knowledge that enable you to do it, then experiment, try things out. Get uncomfortable to become comfortable.

3. **Consistent.** If you say you are something, but don't embody it or do it, people will stop asking you for it and will not associate you with it.

You are consistent when what you say, what you do, and the way you are when you say it and do it are all aligned. People will be clear about what to approach you for, and what not to. What you will say yes to, and what you will turn down. You have an opinion, stand by it. You have a message, stick to it. Your consistency ensures your stakeholder's clarity.

When you are consistent, people will know what they can rely on you for. Priceless.

These 3Cs are the DNA of The BRILLIANT Communicator. They are the bedrock of who you are and how you come across – embodying them constructs confidence.

I don't like the word confidence. It means different things to different people, and can be weaponised, plus it is seldom defined in a way that the criticised party has something specific to work on. For example:

- 'X doesn't have the confidence needed for this, so we won't offer her/him the opportunity.'

- 'Y doesn't come across as confident, so we won't offer him/her the funding.'

Sweeping terms that encompass a wide range of issues don't help, they hinder.

When you embody the 3Cs, you are confident by default. There is no imposter to deal with – instead, there is a specific issue to unpick and build up.

Credible. Comfortable. Consistent. With these 3Cs in your life, you take on life.

The art and science of brilliance

Why do we make certain decisions and not others? Why do we remember certain people and not others? Why do we tune into certain words and phrases, and not others?

There's a science to what we're doing here – a process of logic and rules – and there's an art – the magic of you; your energy and vibe. With these combined, you communicate with impact and gain influence.

The foundational algorithm, the systematic brain-based building blocks of how to do it, will be covered in Part Two. This will include words, structure, voice, and how to bring attention to something key. For now, it's a great stress reliever to know there's a logical system to building your case, because learning a process means it's easy for you to manipulate when you master it.

When I share my templates with top executives, they hold on tight because they immediately see how hours of life and brain-juice will be freed up. The templates set out a process of thinking, fact-finding, and sharing that shifts focus and energy towards elevating the interaction, not freaking out about it.

Then there's the alchemy: the way you speak; how you're going to be when sharing. Marry the algorithm with the alchemy, and you have magic. People will stop what they're doing and tune into you.

This is not about the superficial. These are fundamental building blocks that will transform the way you think, write, and speak. I bring this up because I'm approached by people who want to improve their communication, presentation, or public-speaking skills – and I discover they've been coached by someone who's focused on what I consider to be surface-level stuff.

The more you embody the 3Cs – being credible, comfortable, and consistent – and master the building blocks of The BRILLIANT Communicator, fine-tuning and delivering stakeholder-centric content, the more you'll rock that stage. Wow. Plus, you will lean into being you, not a copy of someone else – and certainly not a product of training by a person who's read the books, got the letters after their name, and that's where their expertise ends.

Embody the fusion of magical influence and tactical precision. Transform into the unique BRILLIANT Communicator and do it your way.

Summary

Embedding an emotion in your stakeholder is your X-factor. To do this, you need to be OK inside and out – because the way you feel influences how others receive you. Inspiring your stakeholder is the ultimate outcome, and it begins with inspiring yourself to show up as your best you.

Marrying the logical algorithm of communication with the art of performing it, while being your unique credible, comfortable, consistent self, means you become The BRILLIANT Communicator that only you can be. This is how interest leads to inspire.

Think. Reflect on the transformative power of inspiration. Consider how your unique insights can spark this, focusing on the core message that drives and aligns with your stakeholder's aspirations.

Write. Create messages that share knowledge and ignite action, crafting words that motivate, uplift, and resonate deeply with your stakeholder's desires.

Speak. Believe in what you deliver, ensure the perspective of the person you want a yes from is at the centre, and aim to transform them, guiding them from interest to inspired action.

In Part Two, we start to assemble the building blocks of communicating with brilliance.

PART TWO
SHARE

Reflect on a time you said something but were not heard. Why do you think this happened?

Your role as The BRILLIANT Communicator is to convince and convert. Your messages are the bridge between your vision and the world, the medium through which your creations and insights come to life, and you gain funding, clients, partners to collaborate with.

Your journey in Part One has equipped you with clarity and conviction in your why. In Part Two: Share, we focus on the how – how to ensure your messages not only reach ears but move hearts and minds. The challenge is closing the gap between concept and final communication – what you transmit and what your stakeholder receives. You are drilling down to The BRILLIANT Communicator's algorithm as a practice.

In Part Two, you will discover the strategy to select words that have impact, embark on embodying your message across diverse platforms, and leverage your voice, presence, and content to captivate and connect. You are transitioning from the sidelines into the spotlight, from chasing to being chosen. Each section in Share ends with key thoughts and a big idea to reinforce the concepts and inspire actionable insights.

Part Two can be summarised in these three points: tuning in, putting out, seeking signals. Plus, embrace your inner comedian – more on this in Chapter Six.

FOUR

L – Listen

B ELIEVE	R EFLECT	I NSPIRE
L ISTEN	L EVEL UP	I NVESTIGATE
A HA!	N AIL IT	T RANSCEND

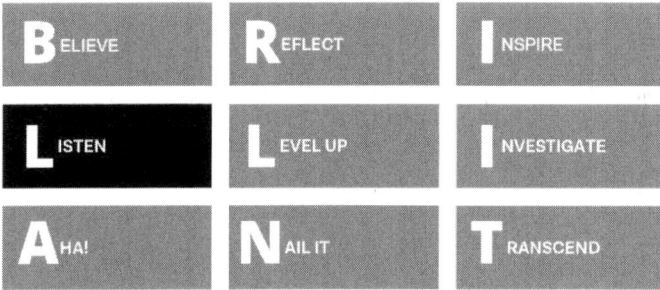

W hy should I listen to you? This is the unspoken thought in everyone's mind. It's often an unrealised one – but it's there.

Your mission as The BRILLIANT Communicator is to transform this barrier into a bridge. The key? Answer this question:

Why should they care?

In Chapter Three, we touched upon this. Your communication must be stakeholder-centric. Here, we'll unpack this and introduce a process that arrives at pertinent, powerful content for you to communicate.

'Who cares?' was a benchmark question the team used when we were deciding which stories to carry and which to ditch during my time with BBC World. We were inundated with press releases from agencies across continents – each vying for a slot for one of their guests on the programme. If we didn't think the topic would be of interest to the potential 300 million viewers globally, albeit prioritising viewers from the region we covered, we dismissed it. Had the public relations and comms professionals pitching their clients thought through this lens, and not the blinkered criterion of pushing their clients' agenda, they'd have increased their chance of making the cut.

Who cares? Why should they care?

Not just passing thoughts, but the critical underpinning of every communication effort. This isn't about doubting your value; it's a strategy to elevate your communication game. It goes beyond hearing what's said. It's about perceiving the unsaid – the underlying currents of emotion, scepticism, curiosity.

This chapter is as much about listening to what is not articulated as it is about responding to spoken words. It's about reading the room, the mood, and the moments of silence that speak volumes. This is about you listening and being listened to.

Let's dive in.

Words – which to use and what to lose

Words have the power to shift thinking, perception, and emotion. I like to think of words as scaffolding that you can hang off, hang on to occasionally – and lean on when you need a moment.

Words ground you. You feel solid and safe when you have the right ones. They liberate. You move around them, you parkour over and under them, and create an experience.

Which are the best words to choose for each occasion? There are 4Ps that enable you to pinpoint the right ones to suit the circumstance: pain, pleasure, priority, and perspective.

People pay attention to pain; they want to eliminate it. When they're pain-free, I call this the pleasure state.

You are the conduit transporting your stakeholder from their pain to their pleasure. To get them tuning into what you're sharing, speak to their priority and perspective, not yours.

What is your stakeholder's pain? What are they losing sleep over? What concerns, mandates, deliverables, issues are their struggle? What is their pleasure state? What do they want to be, experience, feel, achieve?

Know the words they use to describe their pain, pleasure, priority, perspective. Listen – really listen – to their language and phrases. This is what resonates with the person you want a yes from. They notice because it's their lexicon, or because they are words they're primed to notice, words that refer to issues that they must deal with – for example, a global trend, an industry crisis, a target to be hit. Your stakeholder will pay attention because you're using their language and are describing what's on their mind – or the minds of their bosses or the stakeholders *they* want a yes from.

Tune into them, they tune into you.

Tuning into what occupies your stakeholder's thoughts and what's unfolding in their world is about connection, showcasing that you are with them, you understand their issues, and want what they want too. Which is true, because you are creating solutions to take them from their pain to pleasure, outcomes that deliver on their priorities and perspective.

'What words should I use?' is often the primary panicked focus of people who are tasked with communicating something. It doesn't need to be.

Tune in. Interest. Make it easy.

KEY POINTS

- Why should your stakeholder care about what you are saying?
- It's not about what you say. It's about what they hear.
- Make it easy for them to tune in, hear, and resonate with what you're sharing.

The Big Idea: When you follow the steps in Listen, the most important words reveal themselves to you.

Voice – mastering message and impact

Your voice is a vital free tool – it influences what people make of you. We react to voice viscerally – perhaps this has happened to you at some point – but more than that, voice has power over us. For example: research tells us that we tend to trust people

THE BRILLIANT COMMUNICATOR

with deeper voices.[11] This could mean that Margaret Thatcher, the former British Prime Minister noted for her vocal transformation – both elocution and depth – along with her controversial policies, appears in this one instance to have focused on the right thing.

People with deeper voices are paid more too – males, that is.[12] There weren't enough women in the C-suite population to make up a research-worthy sample at the time of the survey.

There's plenty of gender-related nuance in vocal dynamics, but the key point applicable to all is this: a deep voice signals a relaxed larynx, reflecting calm and confidence. Conversely, stress, uncertainty, or nervousness often results in a constricted larynx, producing a higher-pitched, squeaky sound.

Regardless of your pitch, embodying the 3Cs will ensure you sound your best. This is important because speaking – saying words – is a primary way of communicating. As The BRILLIANT Communicator, you do this on stage, on podcasts, when being interviewed, pitching, presenting, at meetings, and even when speaking to yourself (I do this all the time). Speaking is a vehicle for transmitting information externally, and it's a way of transforming information internally.

For example, speaking to yourself out loud is a powerful way to clear your mind and alter your internal chemistry, preparing you for an upcoming interaction.

Think of singing and how it changes the way you feel and the energy you project.

Be remembered for the right reasons.

Here are some considerations when you're approaching speaking interactions to ensure you are heard:

Attention. Pacing. Power. Your authority blooms when your voice does. It's about leveraging the power and pattern of your speech to underline your authority.

Whether you're unveiling a groundbreaking tech invention, pitching a bold business model, or sharing cutting-edge research, your voice is the vehicle conveying it. These are the ingredients to command attention:

Flag. Rhythm. Focus. There's music to effective communication. The crescendos of your voice can spotlight key insights, making them unmissable. It's not only what you say, but how you say it. The rhythm of your speech pulls listeners along, building momentum, guiding them through your narrative with clarity and impact.

Decide which words are key to the idea, emotion, impact you want to embed in your stakeholder. When I'm creating my message, I underline these words to emphasise, to give them an audible energy kick. I give them space to breathe and be effective. Space to settle in people's minds. When I want to pause (silence is powerful, so use it sparingly), I put two lines: / /

Slow down. Nerves can speed up speech, increasing the possibility of you tripping over words and mangling elocution, making it more difficult for people to follow what you're saying.

I used to speak at the speed of light when I first started my TV career. It was as though I had to getitalloutbeforeIforgotit. I was not breathing. I was tense. I was not my true self. Looking back, I likely didn't feel credible. I certainly wasn't comfortable.

You could feel that slowing your speech down makes you more vulnerable. The opposite is true: slowing down allows your brain to speed up. You're creating space for a thought, a connection, a relevant example to pop up on the back of a comment you heard earlier.

If I'm using notes, whether for a talk, an awards ceremony with many names of nominees and winners, or an event that includes introducing videos, calling contributors up to give keynotes, inviting panellists, I have key words for each section, interaction, or thought on a standalone card. This means no turning of pages, no looking for information – it's all accessible at a glance. Consequently, I maintain my rhythm, my flow, and put energy and attention where it's needed. The same can work if you're pitching, presenting – any time you are conveying information.

Vocal warm-ups also help when you're preparing to inspire.

Voice. Mouth. Diaphragm. I like to stand alone backstage before an event kicks off. I hide. The problem with being the chair, host, master of ceremonies, moderator is that people want you to know the answer to all manner of things – 'Where are the toilets?' to 'Where are my notes?' – most of which you don't know the answer to.

In these dark nooks, I have happened upon many a speaker silently stressing. The reasons vary, but the solution doesn't. I've taken a few through belly breathing to bring down their shoulders and their tension, enabling them to think clearly and show up as their best self.

Your voice is not just an instrument; it's a reflection of your inner state. Stress and tension can tarnish its quality. Incorporating vocal warm-ups into your preparation ritual not only enhances your delivery, it also serves as a practice to centre and focus your energy.

Here are a few exercises that help:

- Use **diaphragmatic breathing** to sound more resonant and grounded. Breathe slowly and deeply into your belly, allowing your diaphragm to expand and contract, rather than taking shallow breaths into your chest.

- **Humming** gently warms up your voice and can help lower your pitch. Start with a comfortable mid-range note and gradually move to lower notes. Focus on feeling the vibration in your chest to encourage a richer, deeper voice.

- **Lip trills** – blowing air through closed lips, creating a trill sound while relaxing the lip and facial muscles – reduces tension that can make your voice sound higher. Start with a comfortable pitch and glide down to your lowest note, using your diaphragm to control your breath.

- **Descending scales.** Using vowel sounds like 'ah' or 'oo', sing descending scales starting from a high note down to your lowest comfortable note. Focus on maintaining a relaxed throat and using your breath to support the sound. I recall a famous stage actress who warmed up her voice by saying hip flask repeatedly. Hip was the high note, flask the low. (The contents of said flask likely helped too.)

How you sound is important. Embrace these practices to ensure that when you speak, your audience doesn't just listen – they believe, they follow, they champion your vision.

KEY POINTS

- Warm up your voice.
- How you sound when you express your message is important.
- Prepare and practise what you will say and how you will speak it.

The Big Idea: There's a rhythm to the way we speak. Tap into it and learn how to draw attention to what's important.

Structure and grab attention

There's an often-cited statistic that structured messages are 40% more likely to be accurately remembered by your audience. I have not been able to verify the source, and therefore can't vouch for the figure. Regardless of exactly how much it helps, it helps.

Embrace structure as a guiding principle for effective communication, especially when time is scarce and quick judgements are imminent. Structure organises your thoughts and amplifies your message's impact.

When you have a template in your head, it'll become the way you think – on your feet, in the corridor, at meetings, when you're giving a presentation. You're asked a question, and *boom!* This is how you answer it. Using a simple, clear structure guides your narrative and ensures your message is easy to follow.

You have limited time to make a lasting impact.

My favoured structure is 'What? So what? Now what?' It's simple, effective, and makes you think through pivotal points you need to express, and it's as useful in planned presentations as it is in impromptu speaking scenarios.

Over time, I have modified it to become:

- **What?** Craft the central idea or thought you want to convey, with the stakeholder's pain-free want at its core. It's the answer to: what's the point of this?

- **So what?** Link your message to their needs, challenges, aspirations, or desired outcomes. The question to answer is: why is what you are sharing important to them?

- **Now what?** End with a clear call to action, guiding your stakeholder towards the purpose of the interaction. Make it easy for them to take the next step.

Think of 'What?' as your Tweetable – an attention-grabbing phrase that succinctly addresses the listener's underlying question: 'Why should I listen?' For example, you don't state a new service you're offering; you focus on the impact it has on your stakeholder's business or life.

You could start with a statistic that shares how much time or money is being wasted because of their way of doing things: 'Do you want to save $$$? Hands up if yes. I have news for you!' Frame it in a way that's memorable and shareable, akin to a catchy headline.

Structure and speaker confidence are linked, because the more relaxed you are, the better your recall, and the clearer and better paced your delivery. If you get stuck, move on. Circle back when your brain releases the choice info. Think of structure as your safety net, helping you maintain the flow of your presentation or pitch, while maintaining your inner calm, because you know you'll be OK.

Whether it's in a boardroom, an elevator pitch (imagine finding yourself sharing a lift with a key stakeholder – these things happen), or a global conference, how you structure and deliver your message can mean the difference between being overlooked and being truly heard – and even more crucially, having your message acted on. Marry this with how you use your voice, end on an inspiring emotion, and you are rooted in becoming The BRILLIANT Communicator.

Structure. Recall. Remembered.

KEY POINTS

- Structured message means it's easier for you to recall.
- Structured message makes it easier for your stakeholder to remember.
- Your message is powerful when it resonates, has impact, is remembered and acted on.

The Big Idea: Structure isn't just a framework; it's the foundation upon which powerful, persuasive communication is built.

The secret to being heard

Remember the old school adage, 'I before E, except after C'? Here's my twist for communicators: you must interest your audience before you can engage, entice, or educate them – unless they're already converted to your cause.

Building on Chapter Three about interesting the stakeholder rather than informing them, here we go into more detail and delve into the magic that transforms passive listeners into active participants in your narrative. A vital element is meeting them where they're at – critical because it's easy to forget what it's like not to know something. Plus we as experts have an instinct to educate, to fill every gap in understanding, to rescue, save, convert. Knowledge is a curse if you're not careful.

```
        /\
       /  \
      / Interest \
     /_____\
    /                \
   /     Educate      \
  /_____\
 /                      \
/        Inform          \
/_____\
```

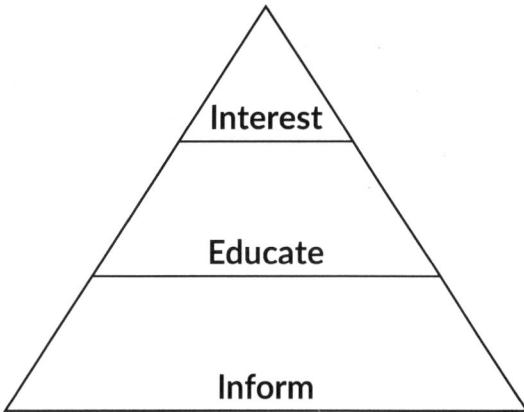

Most people get stuck in the 'educate' part of the Hierarchy of The BRILLIANT Communicator above. This is a problem, because it doesn't spark stakeholder interest, or answer their 'Why should I care?'

Here's an example to showcase the hierarchy. Inform: 'Take this pill at 3pm.' Educate: 'This pill changes X, which makes your Y do Z and your C release D, which it needs for E.' Interest: 'If you don't have enough levels of A, you won't be able to B (something the stakeholder really wants to do). Taking this pill fixes that.' This isn't about withholding information; it's about strategically dispensing information to ignite self-driven exploration. The right people – those who are really invested in B – go on to educate and inform themselves. If you have content that enables them to do this, they're your disciples in the making, and will become your amplifiers and megaphones.

What will interest the person you want a yes from? This is the spark that makes them tune in to you. Transforming the spark into a reason to stay listening – that's the challenge. How you signal and emphasise points helps your audience follow along.

You draw their focus to key elements by using phrases like these:

- This is important because…

- Let me tell you why this is important…

- If there's one thing I want you to know, it is this…

People pay attention because you told them to, so make that next sentence really count.

Your goal is to make it effortless for your audience to tune in and latch on to your message. Our brains are cluttered spaces, buzzing with a million thoughts and bombarded by countless stimuli. You need to stand out and merit attention in that chaos. Make it easy for your stakeholder by moving from being the speaker at the front of the room to becoming the voice inside their head. Spark interest first, then guide them deeper. Tune into their wavelength and make your message impossible to ignore. Transform your communication into connection.

Interest. Entice. Convert.

KEY POINTS

- Meet your stakeholder where they're at.
- Alert them to important things coming up.
- Interest, don't inform.

The Big Idea: Broadcasting your message isn't enough; ensuring it lands with the intended impact is the purpose, whether you're addressing a crowd, a camera, or a colleague.

Own your elephant

'I hope they don't ask me about/notice/bring up…'

We all have our elephants. You need to bring yours up. Own it.

Examples of elephants are things you're asked frequently, based on misconceptions, myths, misunderstandings; thoughts you know people have, but rarely say out loud. They could be because of your age – too young or too old – your gender, or something else to do with you. It could be a past incident that shapes the stakeholder's perception of you. These elephants stand in the way of you getting the yes.

Acknowledging the elephant in the room puts you in a position of power and enables you to move on to things you really want to discuss. Because the issue is no longer an obstacle, it becomes a discussion. This is a great way to deal with bias, pre-formed assumptions, and perceptions of you.

Here are a few ways you can start the conversation:

- You'd be forgiven for thinking…
- I find most people think or assume…
- One thing I'm asked about a lot is…

Call out your elephants clearly and early. Invite them to stand alongside you – tame and tiny, fanning you with their ears.

Elephant. Own it. Power.

KEY POINTS

- Invite your elephants along.
- Introducing them deflates the issue.
- Choose power over panic.

The Big Idea: Listen for the undercurrent in an interaction. No need for confrontation, assumptions, or being squashed by giant elephants.

Summary

You now know how to tune into your stakeholder in a way that tells them you understand them, that you're in it together, and that your successes are one and the same. This shared success narrative is pivotal.

It results in you embodying the 3Cs and being remembered for the right reasons. This increases the chance of your call-to-action being acted on and shared. It means people light up or make a positive mental note when they see your name in print, see that you are a speaker at an event, or even see you in the lunch queue.

You are able to put choice words and phrases they will pay attention to in a flow that makes your message more memorable to them, and to you. You are elevating your status as a known, trusted, and valuable expert in your niche.

Think. Focus on the current pain, pleasure, lexicon of your stakeholder, and consider their unsaid concerns.

Write. Demonstrate with your content that you understand your stakeholder, and are able to meet their wants and needs. Be sure to address the elephants.

Speak. Move from being the speaker at the front of the room to the voice inside your stakeholder's head.

FIVE

L – Level Up

BELIEVE	**R**EFLECT	**I**NSPIRE
LISTEN	**L**EVEL UP	**I**NVESTIGATE
AHA!	**N**AIL IT	**T**RANSCEND

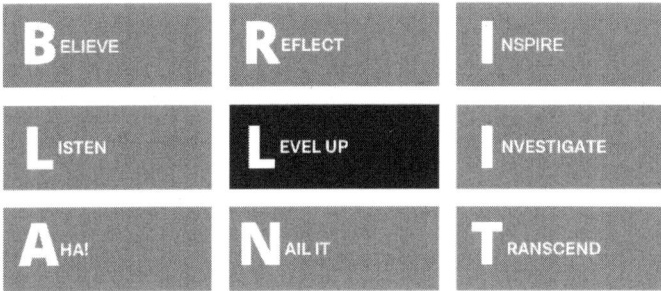

L evel up zeroes in on realities that can derail you and passes on tactics that not only keep you safe but propel your communication prowess.

The outcome of communication is influenced by both your input and the person you are interacting with and includes variables beyond your control. By focusing on your unique perspective and strengths, and what you do control – what you share, how you respond, and how you are when you do this – you increase the chance of achieving the outcome you seek.

Gathering and crafting certain information before interactions is your safety net – resulting in you thriving, not imploding, as you will discover. The message here is: be prepared and never assume.

This chapter is where we delve into elements that make all the difference.

Presence

What is presence? It's a quality that makes people notice you, even when you're not speaking. It's the feeling that you emanate even when you're not there.

Presence is the silent communicator – it is an outer reflection of your inner world.

Central to presence is how you come across – how you are. Your body and what it says is the window into this. You know that your body speaks before you do (see Chapter Three). When what it broadcasts matches what you say, people make more sense of you. This is because the recipient does not focus solely on the words you use; their brain is subconsciously computing everything it can access about you – the way you sound, hold yourself, your energy, how you are, merged with past interactions with you, their observations of your behaviour in various situations, and how they feel when they're around you. All this contributes to an opinion they form about you as an individual, as a professional.

It happens in an instant and it influences what transpires next. With this in mind, ask yourself this question: are words, structure, voice the most important thing?

Yes, because they are your anchor. When you sort out what you're going to say, how you'll say it, and how you'll be when you do so, you feel safer, more credible, comfortable, and in control. This results in your body speaking the right things.

This is not about switching a vibe on when you need something, or when you walk into an important meeting or have a spotlight on you; this is about how you are in general – when you're walking down the corridor, waiting for the lift, having a chat with somebody in the canteen. How you feel on the inside leaks out, people pick up on it, and it shapes what follows.

People with great presence are comfortable in themselves, within themselves, with what they know and do, with what they're wearing, with how they are. They are at ease, and they own their space.

Credible. Comfortable. Great presence.

KEY POINTS

- Your body gives out messages.
- Words are your anchor.
- Presence is about how you come across all the time – not only when the spotlight is on you.

The Big Idea: Own your space. Presence is powerful and is an outer reflection of your inner world. People with great presence are very comfortable – with themselves, within themselves, with what they know, wear, do.

Perception

Right now, somebody somewhere might be talking or thinking about you, making a decision that affects you. It could be whether to collaborate with you or not, to offer you an opportunity or not, to invest in you or not. Do you see? Somebody somewhere is drawing on an impression that they have of you, a perception that they have created about you.

You cannot control the inner workings
of someone's mind – but you can
stack the odds in your favour.

What's worse – a decision-maker getting it wrong by assuming you are capable of more than you currently do and offering you the chance of a lifetime (which you nail), or them believing that you are not the right choice when you really are, your product is better, your expertise is the solution?

People's perception of you is more powerful than your presence. It influences your stakeholder's interactions with you, their thoughts about you, their decisions regarding you.

Perception is about you – what you do and can control – and it's about them – something you cannot control or begin to fathom, because it involves their experiences of people like you, or people they think are like you. It includes their biases, cultural referencing, events in their personal and professional life – all colliding to compromise you or converging to grant you an opportunity.

Boost the chance of being seen as you wish to be seen by clearly communicating what you want, need, and do, and share this at every appropriate opportunity. Critical to this is the third C, consistent. Be consistent in how you show up, what you will and won't take on, what you want to be known for.

For example, if you want to be known for a specific expertise and you're given an opportunity to speak on stage, on TV, or share it in print, but you turn it down, this is not being consistent. Say yes, and then figure out a comfortable way to do it – it's a double whammy if you don't. When you say no, you won't be offered the next opportunity, plus you need to overcome the perception created by your no when you are ready to say yes.

In my broadcasting days, a lot of time would go into tracking down the perfect person to interview about something we were covering. Their credentials, experience, knowledge, published opinion, what people I rate thought of them – all of it came into play. If they said no, I wouldn't waste time approaching them again.

What's more powerful than presence? Perception.

Aligning these two Ps in terms of what you do and want with what others assume and believe about you means breaking free from the confines of misguided opinions about you, and restricting decisions made as a result. Then you will be top of mind when there's a perfect opportunity for you, and you'll be trusted – because you are who you say you are.

In its simplest form, perception can be someone's underlying impression. For example:

'Great person. Can't remember anything they said, but they're brilliant. I must look them up next time I'm in the area, have a related problem, or want them to speak at the event I'm organising.'

Quite powerful, isn't it, the planting of a feeling someone has about you? One that leads to action that serves your 'I made it!'

It can work the other way too: 'I don't like that person. I didn't enjoy that interaction. I don't want to sit through another session with (you).' It might not be a conscious thought, and this is where things become dangerous because it's not necessarily about you, but about the person's inner workings.

Presence and perception are powerful communication tools. Perception becomes reality, because it impacts your lived reality.

Perception. Consistency. Reality.

KEY POINTS

- People's perception of you is more powerful than your presence.
- You cannot control people's assumptions and biases.
- You can control what you do, how you show up, and what you communicate.

> **The Big Idea:** Someone's perception of you easily becomes your reality.
>
> Credibility, Comfort, and Consistency (the 3Cs), combined with a commanding presence, lead to outstanding perception.

Define your difference

Why you? Do you have an answer?

Why should the person whose attention you want listen to you, choose you, pay, hire, seek you out over someone else in your space?

The answer is not your degree, position, or industry. It's the bringing together of what you know, what you do, and how you do it. When these are combined, the nucleus defines your uniqueness and establishes what you are the go-to person for.

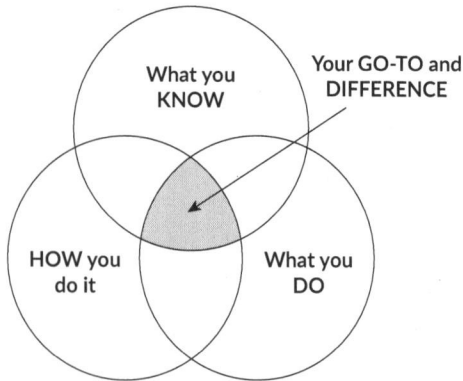

Incorporating what makes you different into your communication pushes away people who are the wrong fit (a great achievement) and attracts the right fit.

Here's a litmus test to see if you're on the right path. When sharing what you do, if your name or your company name can be swapped for a competitor's, and the statement still stands, you have not done the job.

I could have done this with nearly all the guests I've interviewed – substitute their name for that of a competitor, and their answer would work perfectly – especially their first response, which is the most important one, as it determines if a stakeholder will continue listening.

The key to standing out is leaning into your difference. The right type of clients see themselves in what you share, the right stakeholder seeks you out as the solution. However, even the brightest of people don't do this by default.

When I work with clients, I ask simple open-ended questions as a way to benchmark and quickly establish where the client is at in terms of their communication prowess. An example is: 'What do you do?'

The answer is usually generic: 'We are the leaders in this sector/we are one of the top four in the world/ we innovate.'

This means I need to ask for the next layer of information: 'Who seeks you out? At what point? What sort of trouble are they in when they get in touch? Why do they choose you? How is what you do important?'

When I was training the newly appointed country head for a multinational, the initial answer they gave was a generic one. A couple of hours in, it became something quite different:

> 'You know, Nima, the number-one question we are asked is: "How can we continue with our expansion while cutting back on budget?" Governments, the private sector – everyone is dealing with this because of the economic climate at this point. It's not going to change. In fact, it's going to get worse.
>
> 'We are practical first. What do I mean? We do not believe in targets that look good on paper but are not realistic, so we do two things. We go in on the ground with people who shadow teams, and we go big picture, looking at budget constraints and how things can be managed sustainably.
>
> 'In fact, our best client fit is someone who has this exact problem. They trust us because we roll up our sleeves and deliver change alongside them. We do not write up reports, consult, take a fee, and leave. That's not our style of doing business. We are successful only when our clients are sustainable and successful.'

How a person speaks tells me how they think. It informs me of what they have picked up on, have bought into, realise is important. I then gauge how their thinking changes.

You can tell that the person in the example above is picking out key information, organising and cascading it deliberately, experimenting with prioritising client pain, sharing insight and perspective, and embedding outcomes they want to be associated with. It's a far cry from the first answer, which was waffly, boring, and added zero to the conversation. It was peppered with words I ban: leaders, innovative, disrupt, synergy, cutting edge, passion, robust, best practice – the verbal equivalent of a tranquilliser dart. (Trigger alert: 'authentic' is on the list too...) This answer in the example was not the final one we crafted, but it's great as it offers prompts to practise your own go-to and difference:

- The number-one question we are asked is...

- We are... (define a difference)

- We do not believe in... (something prevalent in your industry or that the competition does)

- In fact, our best client fit is...

What's embedded in your ideal stakeholder's mind as a result is: 'Wow, this person or organisation knows their stuff. This is exactly the issue I'm dealing with; I must get in touch.'

Define your difference and state it. It all comes down to this: why you?

Difference. Opportunity. Superpower.

KEY POINTS

- Define your go-to.
- What makes you different is your superpower.
- Spotlight your difference.

The Big Idea: Defining your go-to and difference is the foundation of how to position yourself and communicate in a way that is yours alone. You resonate with the right people and get results.

Facts are your friends

In your mission to convince others of your vision's viability, facts become more than support. They are your foundation for persuasion, your bridge over scepticism; they are your friends. Introduce them into the conversation, lean on them, and in true friend fashion, they will bring out the best in you.

With facts, you not only build stronger cases, but also position yourself as the go-to authority in your domain.

Facts are effective – always.

Facts are your most effective tool for breaking down barriers. If opposition arises when you're negotiating a partnership or seeking investment, introduce hard facts – market research, industry benchmarks, trends and success stories relevant to your proposal. For example:

'Incorporating our solution could (if it truly will, use "will") increase efficiency by up to 40%. This is supported by research I will share in a moment, and is reflected in the results we get working with X clients.'

This isn't a claim; it's a compelling fact-based assertion that commands attention.

Sharing insights that extend beyond your immediate responsibilities or assumed current knowledge showcases your commitment, breadth of understanding, and expertise. It elevates you. For example:

'Current data show 20% sector growth. This is due to the global (state issue, problem, opportunity) and is expected to continue for eighteen months at least because of Y, which means that right now is the perfect time to (your solution).'

Emerging trends and studies, mandates and benchmarks relevant to your ask are great fact friends. They turn 'no' into 'not yet', whereby a rejection becomes a stepping stone. For example:

'Your company's pledge, which you announced in May, aligns with our proposal. Without it, you won't hit your target.'

'You have an obligation to achieve X (your stakeholder's mandate), and your current benchmark is Y (their reality). It cannot happen if you don't do Z (your solution).'

The more stakeholder-specific depth to your fact-driven statements, the more attention you will get, and very likely a call in the future if you don't end up sealing the deal there and then.

To get to the next level, name the specific research, source, study you're citing. This further cements you as a trusted partner in people's minds. Think of it as gaining credibility chips – stack them up. One day, there'll be the occasion to cash some in when you forget or get something wrong.

However, beware of using too many facts, and how you frame numbers. Numbers can confuse, which is why I say, 'Never more than three, no siree.' Too many numbers floating around detract from attention. Plus – and this is key – don't give an absolute number, give it context. Percentages illustrate impact; follow each one up with a reason it's significant. If you rattle off numbers, but do not explain why they are important, what the significance is, why should your stakeholders care?

Context adds to credibility. Your role is to make the right people for your agenda care.

Facts support and elevate.

KEY POINTS

- Facts are your best friends.
- Use facts and stats to support your case and answer questions.
- Sharing facts about things beyond your daily tasks and about your industry and expertise elevates you.

The Big Idea: Embrace facts, keep them close, and invest in your relationship. Stay up to date.

Prepare for the worst

Some situations can derail you if you're not prepared. I'm sharing three here, starting with the issue people tend to be most concerned about in interactive sessions: 'What will they ask me?'

It's not about the question, it's about the answer. Meaning: you can be asked anything; you don't

control that. What you do control is how you are when
you respond – what you say and don't say.

The best preparation for this includes drilling down to
what I call killer questions. For simplicity, let's group
them into three buckets:

- The most frequently asked questions

- The most challenging ones

- What you would hate to be asked or assume you
  will never be asked (never assume)

Here's an example: I was interviewing someone in
the global C-suite of a firm that has been involved
in significant antitrust cases related to monopolistic
practices over the years. The big news (from their
perspective) was their investment in advancing tech-
nological growth in a country marred by very high
youth unemployment. The big news for me was a
mega fine (hundreds of millions of euros) by the
European Commission.

During the interview, I asked questions about the
investment, ensuring we had something to broadcast – and then asked the 'real news' questions. This
is when the interview was stopped by the guest and
the PR entourage, saying they'd run out of time. They
were so fixated on their good news story that they
hadn't considered the obvious questions screaming to
be asked. Classic Kool-Aid moment.

Having ready answers to these questions enables you to feel safe – which will come across in how you show up – and emboldens you to segue into information you want to embed and focus on. Have killer answers for your killer questions. In fact, the more adept you become as The BRILLIANT Communicator, the more comfortable you will be taking the lead with the very first thing you say, which moves away from the problem and being an answer person, to becoming your own spokesperson, framing a question as a gift – granting you space and time to share your big news.

For example, a killer question is asked. Your answer starts with: 'There's a key issue people/regulators/X don't realise…' or 'There's one thing I want you to take on board…' You're expanding on the issue and steering it to what you want to get across. This is not to be mistaken for being evasive – you can circle back to answering the specific issue after your first foray into what you want to share about it. Dealt with this way, killer questions become killer opportunities.

Another worst experience can be being surprised by a question or statement. If you are participating in live interviews – on stage, with the media, on a podcast – you're not in control of what will be said. If you're pitching for funding, you don't know what you could be asked.

The nanosecond post question is when your body can betray you – a flinch, a sharp inhale, or a facial expression that speaks volumes. Take a moment. Breathe.

Say it back to the questioner if you want to ensure you understand. If you want to check what they meant, ask for clarification. If the question is open to interpretation and you're more comfortable with one aspect, dive into that.

If you cannot answer – for legal reasons, or because you're not the right person for it – it's not your forte, or you simply don't know the answer – state this. Then pivot to what you do know, can say, are an expert in. Use it as an opportunity to highlight the key thing you want the right stakeholder for you to know.

Here are ways you can start:

- The first thing I want to say is…

- The one thing I want you to know is…

- The most important point here is…

The third worst-case scenario is losing your audience. Imagine this: you're on TV, on stage, on a podcast, on a LinkedIn live. You've just been introduced. Twenty seconds into your response, there's a major tech fail. No more live.

Satellite interviews were where these mishaps occurred most often in my TV days. These things happen, so consider what you want to get across in your first few seconds. Otherwise, even if there's not a glitch, the person you want a yes from will flip on to another channel or disconnect from what you're sharing if you don't provide a compelling reason for them to listen.

***

Prepare. Pivot. Perform.

***

KEY POINTS

- Create killer answers for your killer questions.
- Stay your comfortable, credible, consistent self, regardless of the situation.
- Start with your most pertinent point to the stakeholder.

The Big Idea: Reframe uncomfortable questions as an opportunity for you to shine a light on the key thing you want to get across.

Summary

'Level Up' zeroes in on enhancing your impact by recognising that effective communication encompasses more than words – it includes how you are perceived, and the assumptions others make based on their lived experience. This chapter shares ways to contain challenges and transmute them into opportunities to communicate your key message. You need this to get you to your next level.

———————————————————————

Think. Reflect on the wider implications of how you show up in your world and the perceptions it creates.

Write. Clarify your unique contributions and difference and add supporting facts. Focus on aligning with your audience's pain, wants, and perspective.

Speak. Take the lead in sharing what you want to embed in your stakeholder's mind, steering uncomfortable interactions to safe territory.

SIX

I – Investigate to Iterate

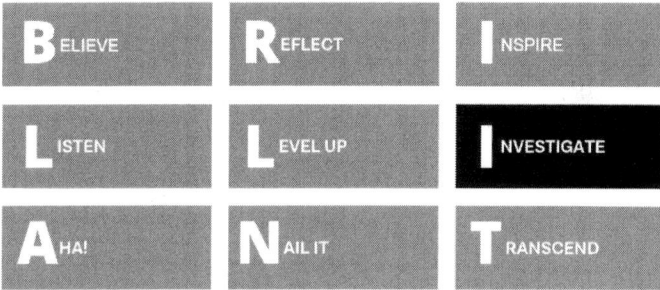

BELIEVE	**R**EFLECT	**I**NSPIRE
LISTEN	**L**EVEL UP	**I**NVESTIGATE
AHA!	**N**AIL IT	**T**RANSCEND

Nothing is perfect, but it does need to be fit for purpose. This chapter enables you to discover whether what you're putting out delivers. It includes revealing what people pay attention to when you communicate, whether your digital footprint conveys what you want to be known for, whether you know and use your current communication mode and media match, and how you can feel fabulous while doing it.

Investigate also shares how you can do all of this at warp speed while cutting out the guesswork. This chapter encourages you to check, tweak, and improve, and reveals that a bit of a laugh over a bit of a cry is optimal.

Explore. Experiment. Experience.

Do you pass the Google test?

Type your name into Google. What do you see? Ideally, you're high up on the first page, if not at the very top! Here's why this matters.

You meet someone, hear someone speaking – on stage, on a podcast, on TV, you read an article they're mentioned in, or even a LinkedIn comment they post – and you're intrigued. You want to know more, what do you do? You Google them.

I do this before meeting a person too. What I find informs ideas, queries, impressions.

Google dictates who
you are to the world.

It's crucial that Google says the right things about you. Are you portrayed as the expert you are? Does your online presence match what you want to do more of? Is the path to working with you clear and easy?

If you don't have a digital footprint, or if there's a mismatch between what you are the go-to person for and what your online presence conveys about you, you will miss out. If you don't have a clear path for ideal clients to find out more, connect with and hire you, you will lose out.

The goal of sharing your expertise is to be easily found by appropriate stakeholders, prompting them to consume your content, absorb the information you're conveying, and ultimately, take the specific action you're requesting – whether it's scheduling a call, arranging a demo, buying your product or signing up for your newsletter.

How can you get Google working for you? Post content – make it useful, quality, and unique to you. Chapter Eight includes how you can take it to the next level.

Visible. Relevant. Engaging.

KEY POINTS

- You are what Google says you are.
- Ensure your digital footprint matches what you want to be known for.
- Have a clear path for stakeholders to take the next step.

The Big Idea: Ensure what's online matches what you offer and how you want to be known.

Feedback loops

Comedians test their material. They don't decide what's funny; they find out from audience reactions during their work-in-progress gigs. As a result, they ditch what dies, tweak what has a signal of interest (a few laughs), and keep what flies (guffaws).

All entrepreneurs, founders, experts, communicators need to do this! I don't mean try stand-up – although they will learn vital skills and experience 'aha!' moments if they do.

People get in touch to work with me after building out a business or product, or honing their expertise, only to realise that their ideal clients aren't aware of them, aren't responding to them, and that they need to raise their profile and be better at sharing what they do. The problem is that they didn't test their material before and while building their 'show', which often results in them wanting to push their product – telling their ideal client what they have created or what their expertise is, desperate for a sale or contract, instead of pulling in the right people for them with curiosity, query, and engagement. What their ideal customers want and think might not fit with the product or sales funnel they've created. It's a scary thought.

Imagine they did this instead: tested what they were doing on their ideal client, incorporating feedback and using the exact words their potential client shares when describing their 4Ps. It's the difference between providing what people want vs imposing what an entrepreneur or expert decides is needed.

If you've created something people don't want, it's better to know, and to know fast. Stakeholder feedback helps mitigate the risk of this. What feedback, comments, or conversations have you had as a result of your output? You're looking for interactions with stakeholders you need or want a yes from, not friends, colleagues, family.

Discovering if and how you're resonating with your ideal stakeholder is how you know your product is viable. Your product could be your expertise and building up a credible 'brand you'. Do you test and share, tweak and test again?

Test your message – because it's not about what you say or put out; it's about what others pick up on. When you nail your message, what you say and what the stakeholder hears will match up.

Here's how you can do this:

- **Benchmark:** Gather data that reflects existing thinking, for example, using a survey, quiz, or a show of hands.

- **Feedback:** Discover information that reflects how, or if, your interaction changes the way your stakeholder thinks about a specific issue.

The key is not to prime people – don't let them know you're going to ask them about your talk, message, or interaction. Priming messes up results, because people pay attention in a different, more deliberate way. Reframe interactions as a work in progress – an opportunity to refine your communication skills and gather essential data. Don't solely rely on gig feedback. Instead, prepare by testing the most critical part of your content – your opening statement – in advance.

I have a simple method with no need to gather information beforehand. You say something like, 'I'm creating a piece about my thinking on A. Can I share it with you?'

You speak it. Then you ask for the three words the stakeholder remembers and the big idea they take away. If you're interacting with a group, after you say your piece, hand out pen and paper, or get the stakeholders to use their phones, and ask them to write down the three words and big idea. If they speak them, they will influence and contaminate each other's thinking.

Pre-gig feedback on your opening lines is essential. It sets the tone and determines whether your stakeholder will want to know what comes next. Different people tune into different elements of what you're sharing, because their referencing, experiences, pain points, wants, and needs vary. Ask enough people and you'll get a feel for what stands out. Ask the right type of stakeholder for you, and you'll gather pertinent information.

What do they notice? Is it because it's a word they're primed to pick up on, or because you emphasised that word?

Tweak, try again. Your message will never be perfect. It's a continuous process of explore, experiment, experience.

Don't decide; discover what works.

KEY POINTS

- Does what the stakeholder hears align with what you want to convey?
- If not, tweak and repeat.
- You will notice patterns in what people pick up on and how you can direct attention.

The Big Idea: When you nail your message, what you want to instil and what the stakeholder realises will match up. The next section shares how you can do this on steroids.

Borrow while you build

'I'm an IT guy – I'll write a few blogs and become known.'

I disagree with this approach, and you should too. Here's some context.

This person is highly specialised, managing systems for a global financial exchange. After a decade in his current role, he wants to work for himself. It's time to broadcast his expertise to the right audience.

Instead of going down a hole and blogging – his zone of familiarity – which means directing people to the posts (effort) and waiting to discover what resonates (taking time), he'll get much more out of being a guest on the right podcasts. This is because he will discover how to explain his go-to and difference more fluidly, and he will quickly learn what resonates with his ideal stakeholder. Feedback can be in real time if the podcast is live and includes a question-and-answer (Q&A) session.

Borrow while you build, as long as you're addressing the right audience for you. Here's what I mean: discover podcasts and communities that serve your ideal stakeholder avatar – ones that align with your vibe and values. Guest on these podcasts and host Q&A sessions for members in these communities.

This approach is effective on various fronts. It sharpens how you hone, structure, and convey your messages. It helps you understand challenges people face related to your expertise – these might not be what you think – and it reveals your own communication hurdles, while starting to uncover your signature phrases and words. Plus – and this is a power move – it highlights what people pick up on and start realising from what you share. It's supercharged feedback.

This is your 'How do I resonate?' phase. Do not mistake it for marketing yourself. The focus is on improving as a communicator; the bonus is that you market yourself or offer by default.

This approach has other advantages too, including establishing relationships with key contacts and potential clients at speed – invaluable. Plus, speaking your knowledge enables you to formulate thoughts that you can then disseminate via your preferred media match.

I like to frame this process with 3'I's that are in fact three steps. First comes information: figuring out what to share, where and how. Then there's discovering what resonates with the right people for you, which leads to iteration. Once you know what resonates with your people, and become comfortable sharing, you move on to mastering output through implementation.

Information. Iteration. Implementation.

When you build on solid foundations, you move forward faster. Doing it by borrowing audiences, while figuring out what you will communicate, and how, is the closest you'll get to pushing the boulder downhill.

Leverage. Engage. Iterate.

KEY POINTS

- Borrow the right audience.
- Discover their challenges and aspirations.
- Learn your way of putting things.

The Big Idea: By sharing your message with your ideal audience, you discover what influences your stakeholder to take the action you want. Cut out the guesswork. Cut down time needed for feedback. Discover, don't decide.

Fear to fab

What are you scared of?

Becoming known for your brilliance means saying yes when there's an opportunity to showcase and share, pitch and present. On stage, on the page, on TV, in the power broker's room, or by borrowing a podcaster's audience. It can be intimidating. What are your concerns, and what is at the core?

This section is the result of being invited to train a government minister who was embarking on a tour where he'd be on stage, interviewed, and hosting events during a roadshow. When I asked what his biggest worry was, his answer gave me an 'Aha!' moment:

There is a root fear – a fear at the centre of potential apprehension.

This is not to say that it's the only dread. I know people who are physically sick at the thought of speaking on stage. This is not what I'm delving into. I'm reflecting on the origin of declared fears for most people.

- 'I don't know what questions they'll ask me.'

- 'What if I forget?'

- 'Will I sound clever?'

These are some of the worries that people I've worked with have voiced. They are the by-products of this terror: looking like a fool.

No one wants to be considered a fool. The higher up the ladder you are, the more known you are, the more there is riding on the interaction, the more you have to lose – or so it feels.

You could feel like a fool if you forget a key point, a fact; if you're not aware of news just out that's significant to your industry. Here's a dose of reality. You *will* forget something at some point, something important. There will be a fact that you actually know, but can't recall in the moment. It's not a matter of if you will be taken aback by a statement, question, or concern – it's a matter of when. You don't need to look or feel like a fool when it happens. What people will remember is how you handle the situation.

It's tough if you're not at ease with a literal or metaphorical spotlight on you. To help address this, define the issue and break it down to mini parts.

For example, does the feeling of trepidation hit you when you look out at a sea of faces staring back expectantly? Is it the thought of hundreds or thousands of people tuning into the podcast you're a guest on and hearing what you say in perpetuity? Is it letting go of notes that have become a crutch you clutch on to? Perhaps forgetting your flow is the worry.

Knowing the exact issue you're dealing with means you can do something about it. It is different for each person. I call this my DB2B: define it, break it down to build it up. Works a treat whatever the issue.

Build on solid foundations, be your 3C self and take a moment to breathe. Relax your body, face, brain, and proceed. When I shared tactics to keep the minister centred and remaining his 3C self, it liberated him from his specific concerns and the fear of coming across as a fool. The same applies to you.

Fool. Fear. Fab.

KEY POINTS

- Identify your main concern.
- Break it down into 'this is what I can do about it.'
- People will remember how you handle a situation, not every word you say.

The Big Idea: It's human to be concerned about facing the media, a panel, an audience – especially when a lot depends on it. It's not about what happens, it's about how you handle it.

The power of what you *do* know

To excel in your niche, you must possess encyclopaedic knowledge. Myth.

This mindset is a barrier to your next success. It's not about what you don't know. It's about what you do know. Brilliance isn't having all the answers, it's mastering the art of engagement and sharing what you know right now.

Many experts and entrepreneurs feel they must offer PhD level value. They spend hours of their life filling knowledge gaps with information they believe will boost their credibility and kudos – while putting off doing the one thing that'll move them forward: sharing what they already know to be true.

If this is you, stop. You know enough. You know what you know and it is valuable. Otherwise, no one would ask you questions, seek you out, want your input, opinion, product, system.

In fact, you want to be only slightly ahead of those you serve – if you're miles ahead, you're not relevant to them. For example, I overheard two people talking about a poster on a wall. It was advertising a yoga class that was going to focus on handstands. The image was a graphic of someone standing on one hand, the other extended to his side. The two people commented that there was no way they could achieve anything like that, so they were not going to go.

I asked the person running the class if he was aiming to have people stand on one hand. He wasn't. He was losing out because the unrealistic image conveyed that the class was too advanced for most potential stakeholders, his client base, to get joy or value from going.

Meet people where they're at, and work with what you know and have got. The right people will want more from you.

When it comes to putting out your content, don't buy expensive kit or software. Don't buy anything. It becomes a distraction. The only thing you want to do is create output in the most hassle-free way for you with what you already have. You're building a communication process and system to fit in with your unique life and how you function.

You have something that you can use right now as material – or use with minimum tweaks. It could be a method or message that you take team members or clients through, or a document that outlines this. Break it up into usable bits and put it out in your most comfortable format. For many, this is a written LinkedIn post.

Make it easy. Reuse what resonates. For example, record audio of a written post that generates feedback, comments, or direct messages. Record a video of yourself sharing the same information. Define your next communication medium, and repeat.

Let's not get ahead of ourselves, though. Creating more output in additional formats isn't necessarily the answer if the question is: how can I become known for the right thing by the right people? We'll touch on this in Part Three, which is coming next.

Share. Engage. Enlighten.

KEY POINTS

- What you know right now is enough.
- Don't be too far ahead of your ideal stakeholder.
- Put out your current brilliance.

The Big Idea: Share your lived experiences that solve your stakeholder's problems. Offer your insights. Don't get hung up on what you don't know.

Summary

Explore. Experiment. Experience. Investigate to iterate involves taking ownership and responsibility for your digital footprint and communication evolution. Ensure that what you do and want to do more of is aligned with how you show up online. Embrace and celebrate communicating what you know, refining your message through real-world feedback in a way that includes and increases your audience base, while exploring and noting what stakeholders take away from their interactions with you.

Three things to note from this chapter are:

- Meet yourself where you're at.

- Work with what you've got.

- Borrow while you build.

This is about you. Your life. Your reputation. Your credibility.

The big takeaway from Part Two is: the buck stops with you. In Part Three, Elevate, we dive into how you can transition to the next level.

Think. Reflect on how you can evolve your communication style to better connect with your stakeholder, and how you can experiment with ease. Frame it as your work-in-progress gig.

THE BRILLIANT COMMUNICATOR

Write. Document your insights, the feedback and results as you try out different ways of sharing what you know to be true.

Speak. Focus on conveying what you do know. Develop your performance by borrowing a relevant audience.

PART THREE
ELEVATE

I want *you*.

Prepare to deepen connections, wield influence when you communicate, and refine your public persona. This section uncovers tactics to keep you on track and achieving your purpose when you communicate, and ways to turn unplanned interactions into opportunities that solidify you as a recognised leader and authority in your field.

'Elevate' is your guide to shaping narratives, magnifying your impact, and transforming your vision into collective realities. Get ready to step into your inherent value, establishing yourself as the singular, indisputable choice in your domain, the only choice, and building your category of one.

SEVEN

A – Aha!

BELIEVE	**R**EFLECT	**I**NSPIRE
LISTEN	**L**EVEL UP	**I**NVESTIGATE
AHA!	**N**AIL IT	**T**RANSCEND

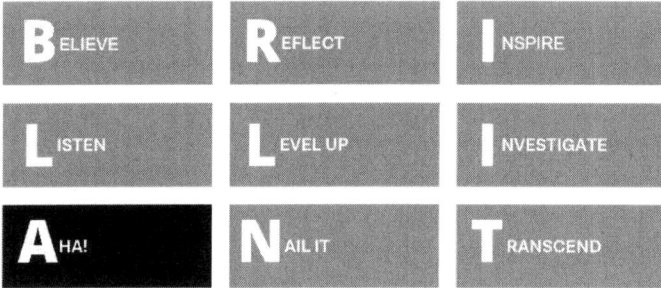

A re your messages important? They're important to you – but are they important to the person you're communicating with, the stakeholder you want a yes from? That depends.

You now know that aligning your messages with stakeholder perspective, pain, priority, pleasure gets them interested and defines the value of the interaction for them. You also know how easy it is to end up adding information that's important to you, but results in stakeholder disconnect. How can you ensure that you stay on track, fulfilling the purpose of your interaction, and leaving people delighted to have discovered you and thinking: 'I'm so glad I heard / read / saw that.'

***

Be guided by your 'Aha!'

***

Astonish with insight

The reason experts and world leaders were invited on to the programmes I presented was sometimes for their name appeal, but always for the insight and opinion their status and experience offered (I hoped). During the interview, I'd look for something that stood out – something that told me (and the millions tuning in) how the issue being discussed was important and the impact it had on people, life, business.

This section enables you to do a better job than many of these guests.

Delivering on your agenda – the purpose of the interaction – only happens when you provide the stakeholder with something they will value. To make it easier for you to do both, embrace upside-down thinking, and be guided by your 'Aha!'

First, define an 'Aha!' you want to convey, such as 'Aha! I didn't realise X' or 'Aha! I get Y now'. It is the insight, thought, or perspective you know to be true and aim to instil in your stakeholder's mind.

For example, this is what I hope to instil in your thoughts as the result of reading this book:

> 'Aha! I now realise that being The BRILLIANT
> Communicator is the surest, shortest path to
> my success. It means I will become known for
> my expertise, grow and scale my business,
> attract the right clients and opportunities,
> and reclaim my freedom and time, because
> I will know how to get the yes I'm after. I feel
> relieved and less anxious about the future.'

Determining the outcome you want your stakeholder to realise before you construct your piece enables you to evaluate what you create against it. Does what you're sharing reinforce it or detract from it?

Earn attention.

Your opening line, also known as your hook, needs to work hard. Craft it to capture attention, which is fleeting. Framing it as 'earning attention' can help, as it encourages you to deliver value and relevance that keep your audience engaged and eager to hear what you'll share next. A sure-fire way to achieve this is to ruffle some feathers!

You have an opinion, a contrarian view, a contentious take on something that is important to the person you want a yes from. You arrived at it when you extrapolated data, insight, information, experience, and joined dots in a way that is unique to you, because you are the only person with your life's trajectory.

State it. Say it first. It keeps the right people sticking around and leaning in to what you share next.

People are often reluctant to ruffle feathers – they don't want to risk alienating or losing out on a potential client or contract. The opposite is true: do this, and you attract the right people.

As you continue with the rest of what you share, ensure you include answers to the two questions I have asked most in life:

- Why is this important?

- What is an example?

I call this closing the loop. You close your communication loop when what you convey does not beg for obvious follow-up questions from the stakeholder's perspective. Including answers to them in your opening statement ramps up interest and positions you as an authority to be reckoned with.

For example, if you are revealing a report, a study, or findings of some sort, start with what surprised you, your opinion about it, your thoughts and insights, what you believe this means, and what's important to note. Answering 'Why should they care?' with the stakeholder's 4Ps in mind – pain, pleasure, priority, and perspective – is your winning formula.

Most communicators tend to be answer people, sharing 'what we did' and 'how we did it' information. You can get on to that if it's needed, but no one will be listening if you start in this bland way. Go in bold. The concept of upside-down thinking helps. Instead of following a typical report or document structure – setting up points, presenting lots of information, summarising at the end, or including background, reasons, and methods – flip it. *The start* is where you deliver your big moment. A closed communication loop becomes an opportunity loop. To help, I share a simple structure I use for crafting videos in Chapter Eight.

Think upside down to astonish and awe. Define and stick to your 'Aha!' for results.

Always be pitch-ready

I was on a train, heading to a meeting at a conference, when I thought, 'What if one of the speakers doesn't show up? I could step in, save the day, collate data and feedback, and make right-person-for-me connections.'

I created the skeleton for a fifteen-minute talk. I figured out the start and the end, and the action and outcome I wanted from it, planning to fill in the middle with what was relevant to the room. I'd get a feel for this by snooping around beforehand and having chats. By snooping, I mean discovering what's on people's minds, their worries and relevant elephants.

Imagine what it would feel like to have the organisers of an event gushing over you – amplifying you, your brand and presence because you saved the day. Would you dare to do it?

The impact of readiness includes the organiser knowing they can depend on you and owe you one, plus an audience in awe and wanting to have a conversation with you – at least to ask: 'Wow! How did you do it?' Always be pitch ready.

It's not about memorising every word. It's about marrying what your stakeholder in the room is interested in with what you are all about. The perception of you will be off the scale as a result – for all the right reasons.

Opportunities present themselves – are you ready to step up and embrace them? Predetermining an 'Aha!' you'd like to instil in your ideal stakeholder before you go to an event helps – whether you're scheduled to speak or not.

I'd go further. Have a thirty-second, fifteen-minute, and thirty-minute outline of what you want to get across in your head. Yes, you can. Good things will happen.

Be obsessive

What is your stakeholder *really* obsessed with? How can you share these obsessions in a way that makes them feel seen? This is beyond pain – it's about how they live, what they like, avoid, buy, vent about.

Demonstrate that you know them, hear and see them, understand and get them.

> Aim for the bullseye: your
> stakeholder's obsession.

The more you speak to narrow audiences in a language they understand, sharing quirks and beliefs, the more connected you become. For example, imagine you're speaking at a convention for accountants, dentists or food manufacturers – whoever your best clients are. What are two fascinating things you know about this group of people?

Bubble gum was invented by an accountant.[13]

Mick Jagger of The Rolling Stones and Robert Plant of Led Zeppelin were training to be accountants before their music careers took off.[14]

The first recorded dentist lived in 3000 BC. Hesy-Ra, renowned as a tooth expert, lived during the Third Dynasty of Egypt.[15]

Dentists' stress levels are through the roof – a 2019 study found that half those surveyed said that it affected their practice.[16] Perhaps your product helps lower it.

A food colourant called carmine is made from crushed insects.[17] It was used to colour red Skittles until 2015. Do you regret eating them?

In 2011, *Time* magazine reported that cheese was the most stolen food – around 4% of all cheese manufactured.[18] This could be because it goes with everything, or because eating cheese triggers happy hormones.[19] Parmigiano-Reggiano has even been used as a bank deposit in Italy – so this works for a banking or finance audience too.

These examples can be considered silly – are they? They're interesting to specific people, change the energy in the room, could get a laugh! Being obsessive is about more than the pain your stakeholder is in; it's about things to do with them, common ground, culture, in-jokes, things that light them up – with joy or with fury. You become part of the tribe – a guest, not an intruder. Perhaps even one of them – trusted and welcomed.

Needy equals no

The most powerful way to show up is 'I am'. The sexiest energy to have is 'with you or without you'.

A client advanced beyond initial pitches to the final funding round for her business for the first time by embracing this. It happened when she moved from a conditional mindset – 'When I get X, I will be (insert position, expertise, company you're launching, thing you want to be known for)' – to 'I am the go-to person and business for (insert expertise, product, process).'

Own your space. You are the expert right now – radiate 'with you or without you' energy. Here's what I mean. You're launching your business, your product, or implementing your process regardless of whether the person you want a yes from grants it. Frame it as hosting a party and handing out invites. It makes people want to be there. Desperate to be there even, because they don't want to miss out.

'This is happening, with you or without you,' versus 'I can only do this if you choose me.' Check in with yourself when you're pitching, planning, presenting. How are you framing your thoughts, and how are you positioning yourself? Needy equals no. Cultivate 'I am' and 'with you or without you' energy. It'll take you places.

Plant your word-tree

If people forget everything you say, what one thing do you want them to remember? Define it. This is your tree trunk. Then distil everything you want to get across into three key words – I have done this in various chapters to familiarise you with what I mean. These are your branches.

Next, define a maximum of three facts, stats, examples, or points related to each keyword, and whittle the information down to one word for each. These are your twigs. This means you have twelve words to remember in total, plus one main point or idea.

Make a word-tree and see how your thinking flows and fits together.

You can draw from your memory bank to add depth and support, enriching and expanding your message as needed.

Make it three words, yes that'll do, so it sticks in your mind just like glue.

3.2 Support

3.1 Support

3.3 Support

1.3 Support

1.2 Support

#3 Key Word

1.1 Support

#1 Key Word

2.1 Support

2.2 Support

#2 Key Word

2.3 Support

The One Thing Stakeholders Remember

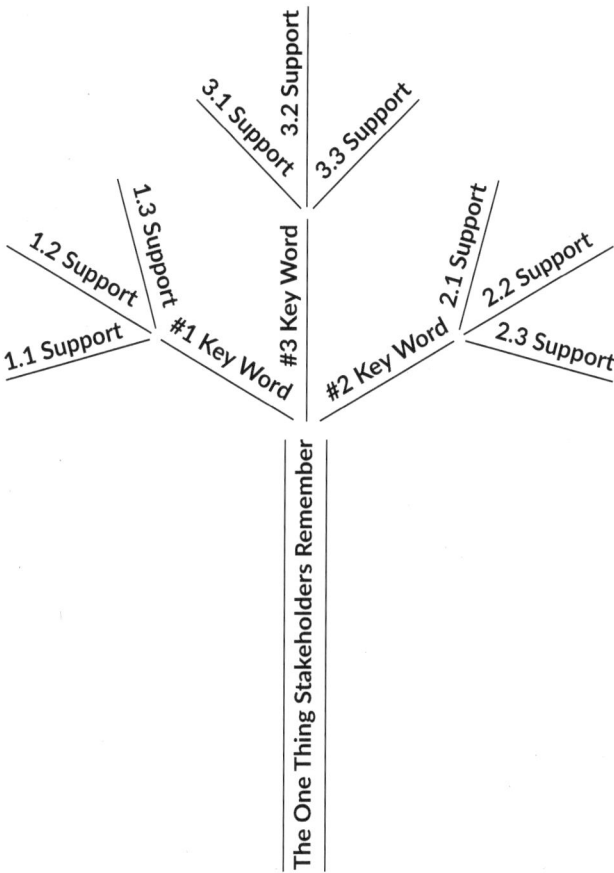

Your word-tree becomes the way you think and link information in an instant. Learning to arrive at one word that brings a concept or idea to life is a magnificent skill. Give it a go! Plant your word-tree. Grow interest.

Using these key words in your message – whether at the beginning by stating, 'This is what's important:

word one, two, three,' or at the end when summing up – helps your stakeholder remember and retain the information too. Here are more tips to help you master becoming The BRILLIANT Communicator:

- **Stand.** If you are speaking – in front of a group of people, on stage, in a meeting, virtually – stand if you can. The way you come across is different. Your energy and presence are elevated. Some conferences I moderate arrange things so that interactions are seated. I stand. Panellists can sit; I stand when I chair, moderate, speak.

- **Don't give Google.** I beg people I train not to give me Google – information I can easily look up. Your gold is your insight, gut, opinion. This is what sets you apart. Think of Googleable information as padding, buffer. It doesn't showcase your insight, experience, opinion. It does nothing to promote unique you.

Going back to the idea of closed communication loops and communicating complete thoughts, I'd like to pass on one more thing. A fabulous closed communication loop is one that can be used in its entirety as a fully formed compelling statement. Thinking and sharing in this way means you leverage opportunities because your message can be lifted from an interaction and used elsewhere. In my TV days, I loved it when someone said something pithy and fully formed that could be used as a headline and as part of a main interview in one programme, then used again as a sound bite (shorter statement) in a report for a different programme.

There are other benefits too. When you communicate in complete loops, you are more in control of what's put out, because there is no need for editing. It leads to you becoming known for your superior communication skills that save people time, energy, effort. You are more sought after as a result, and your message, brand, credibility and authority are magnified.

When you're crafting your complete communication loop, your word-tree is an invaluable tool. When you include the elements of the word-tree in what you communicate, it makes it easier for your stakeholder to remember key information too.

Summary

Communication equals opportunity. 'Aha!' shares strategies to ensure your interactions deliver on their purpose, on purpose. A central pre-defined takeaway becomes the measure of what to include and what not to, ensuring you attract attention and grow interest, resulting in the right people for you taking action.

Mastering this tactic enables you to quickly leverage interactions – be they planned or spontaneous.

Think. Identify the 'Aha!' you want to convey.

Write. Craft your message with careful consideration of word choice and information to ensure clarity, credibility, impact, fulfilling your 'Aha!' and closing the loop.

Speak. Deliver your message with the focus on cascading and growing interest, enabling your audience to easily arrive at the 'Aha!' Make it so intriguing and relevant, they discuss it over a coffee with their peers.

EIGHT

N – Nail It

BELIEVE	**R**EFLECT	**I**NSPIRE
LISTEN	**L**EVEL UP	**I**NVESTIGATE
AHA!	**N**AIL IT	**T**RANSCEND

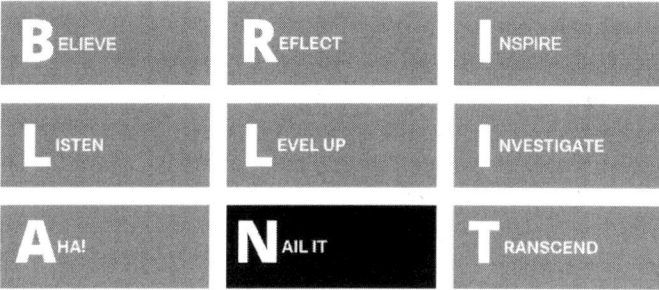

In 'Nail It', we dive into turning potential communication pitfalls into platforms for success. It's about stopping the cycle of missed opportunities due to overlooked detail, and moving from navigating the pressure of sudden attention from the powerbrokers of your future to ensuring your message is heard loud and clear.

This chapter is a trove of insights for standing firm when the ground seems to give way beneath you. Reframe every interaction as participation. Discover templates to raise your profile and become a spotlight pro.

Preparation and practice
make you persuasive.

Stop losing out.

Sh!t happens

You've been invited to a coveted meeting of powerful people. They are demigods in your field and your future – if they buy into you. Acceptance by them opens doors.

You're sitting there, smiling, soaking it all in, when without notice, you're invited – publicly – to the stage to speak about what you do. Will it be mic drop, or… mic flop?

This really happened. Someone became my client when he realised that it could have been so much worse, or better.

He sent me a series of pictures taken by the official photographer. The first shows him beaming in a pinch-me moment. Next you see a quizzical look on his face, and then he's on stage, microphone in hand, with a giant backdrop that has the key word he's expected to zone in on (related to his expertise), resplendent and right in your face. I wonder if the photographer had a heads-up…

My client pulled through and made it to the next level. Phew.

You don't get a second first impression.

Imagine this happening to you. It's one thing volunteering to fill a speaker slot, another to be spotlight-punked, with your peers and superiors waiting expectantly. However, it's fair game if you want to be known for your expertise. In fact, it's an unparalleled opportunity to showcase your brilliance.

Spotlight-punked or spotlight-pro, the choice is yours. Two things will keep you safe: crafting the 'Aha!' you want to instil before any gathering or interaction, and going with the flow. Let me expand.

The more events you participate in, the increased probability that something will go wrong at some point. It could be that notes vanish, slides (don't do Death by PowerPoint) aren't compatible with the tech, videos don't play, the person tasked to help is a liability, you forget something key.

No one knows what you had planned. Let go of what could have been and embrace what is. People only know what you put out. What they experience in your presence.

When things fall apart, you don't.

The BBC episodes I presented were seldom what was planned. They were what happened. People pulled out, locations were rubbish, guests didn't bridge the information gap.

My cameraman and I once flew for 8.5 hours to interview a character on location. Him rocking up in his red Ferrari (totally inappropriate for the terrain... a sign of things to come?) to a spot in the Moroccan desert, with barren landscape as far as the eye could see, and sharing plans for a sovereign-wealth funded property multiplex was to be the opening shot eye candy – in our minds.

The guest never showed up. That was a particularly doomed trip, which was turned around by us focusing on 'What can we do?' not what had gone wrong. It was one of the best episodes we broadcast.

On stage, at meetings, during a pitch – it's all about how you deal with curveballs, how you are. It's about what the audience can see, hear, feel – not what's missing. They will never know, unless you fall apart, become stuck, or point it out.

If you need a moment, stay your calm, comfortable, brilliant self and introduce a fact, fill a gap with some-thing relevant from your obsession list, or share an answer to a killer question. These are your leaning posts, the stepping stones around your word-tree (see Chapter Seven). They lift your energy and are a life-line. Frame it as a distraction that is fail-safe – your stakeholder leans in, your brain un-blips, you feel powerful and in control.

I mitigate all manner of risk by reading around issues, topics, people speaking, and am a vault of... you could say useless information, but boy does it help. Things to fill time while tech is fixed or a speaker is found, to distract from problems, to change up the energy if a speaker has been boring, or simply to have a memo-rable conversation during a break. Plus all the seem-ingly disparate information settles to form links with existing and future knowledge. Dots are connected, ideas are formed. It morphs into fodder for insight around overheard comments or conversations. Ways of thinking that add to your take, your value.

Make like a Scout: be prepared. Your brain and breath-ing relax, your tension and cerebral searching fall away – the words will come. You will own your space and the room.

This is not to say that you must never convey that you've forgotten something, or something has gone wrong. It's all in how you do it.

Always be prepared to shine a light on what you know and do in a memorable, relevant way, which is what we'll explore next.

Bring it together

Surprise! Let's start with the example in the previous section – you're in a room with powerbrokers of your future, and with no warning, and zero time to prepare, you're spotlight-punked.

How can you navigate this? First, define the major challenge the people in the room face. You will have gleaned this from side conversations, overhearing chat, previous speakers or topics raised, the titles of the talks, the title of the event. Zoom in on your take on this, your perspective and insight. Focus on what you do and know that's different – for example, you are customer-facing and understand the concerns and frustrations of your stakeholder's clients, or you speak the local language and know the culture and the undercurrent.

Using 'What? So what? Now what?' as your prompts reduces mental pressure and means you can pepper your message with information that highlights 'I do this' over 'I know this'. State what's obvious to you and keep it simple. For example: 'When we do this X happens. Our work demonstrates that clients prefer Y.'

Think Tweetable, so your point
is not deletable.

Lifesavers include interacting with the audience by asking questions and encouraging a show of hands for answers, naming the elephant in the room, and if you're feeling powerful, saying the thing you don't think you can say because it might alienate or shock. Do it, as long as it's based on your credibility, experience, authority. Take in the ripples of reaction and take note of who wants to connect with you as a result (your best client, stakeholder or champion).

This might seem like a lot to process quickly, but the more you apply The BRILLIANT Communicator tactics, the faster your thinking synthesises inputs – issues, nuance, and the key to capturing interest. Processing information and crafting how to communicate with impact and authority becomes your default mode, your operating system.

Thinking through an 'Aha!' is a useful exercise to do before any interaction and will enhance every exchange. When you're prepping for a scheduled engagement, familiarise yourself with what you want to share to the point where the opening and closing lines are etched in your mind, enabling you to start strong and conclude with power – looking across the room, not down at notes or prompts.

Experiment and be daring with how you start:

- Your biggest fear is… (speaking directly to your stakeholder).

- X% of you believe Y, our data tell us Z (a shocking difference).

- Why is nobody talking about A (the elephant or a major issue)?

Generate next-level intrigue with: 'Can I tell you a secret?' or 'Do you want to hear something completely wild?'

Approach interactions with curiosity and as an opportunity to discover, not dictate; a chance to speak with, not at. Frame interactions as participation – and be prepared.

Fatima, a client, nailed your new way of thinking when she shared: 'I now think: if someone asks, "What did Fatima say?" what do I want the answer to be?'

The next section helps you master this.

Template and tips

Here is a simple structure I use to clarify and include key information when I'm writing a video script. You can use it to create any type of communication, content, or interaction. Notice that populating it requires bringing together all the elements we've covered so far.

Consider the sections as prompts for detail. You don't need to follow the order it's laid out in; I like to start with what's easiest, expanding on different segments and incorporating examples or data tailored to how, where, and for whom it'll be used. I have filled in the template with an example as a guide.

Aha! statement: The Big Idea you want to plant in your stakeholder's mind

This is the yardstick to check your communication delivers on its purpose. You don't say this; it's what your stakeholder concludes based on what you share. Defining it helps you stay focused on what fulfils your goal.

Aha! After watching this, I understand that highlighting my unique value and what sets me apart from the competition is key to building my credibility, authority, and client base. I will have the attention of the right client for me, which means I spend less effort qualifying and converting.

This means my energy goes on serving the right people, and that the right stakeholders are in my circle and pipeline. They will convert to clients when they're ready. Win! My business will grow, I will stay sane.

Headline options, to use as a title for your talk or as the title of a YouTube video, for example

[Statement] Don't chase clients. Do this instead.

[Gain or positive] From chase to chosen – how being an authority puts you in power.

[Loss or negative] Why fitting in means you lose out.

Hook or Tweetable: this is how you start your opening statement

If your ideal client *believed* you could solve their problem, how easy would it be for you to make money?

Problem

There are only two ways to get paying clients:

- You reach out to them.
- They reach out to you.

Most businesses operate in the first category.

You might be brilliant at what you do. So what? Your ideal client doesn't know and doesn't get in touch.

You are not a known authority, your credibility footprint is non-existent.

Pain

As a result, you're wasting thousands on marketing and cold outreach, just to access and convert a single lead. All the time worrying where the next client will come from. All the time burning through time and money.

Pleasure

Instead of this, imagine that clients reach out to you. It's a powerful position to be in. No more chase. Instead, you're chosen.

How can it happen?

Empathy or authority

I have never applied for a job. I've worked with global organisations by invitation, because a decision maker knew me, or knew about me, and got in touch. My clients include the UN, UNDP, BBC, Accenture, PwC, Forbes Arabia, FT, governments – you get the picture.

It's a totally different relationship when someone seeks you out because they know you are the solution.

How can this be your reality? Here is the one thing you must do if you want this for yourself:

Process or steps

Be known for your expertise.

Sounds simple. How?

Get speaking, writing, sharing your thoughts, insight, and point of view. Put out your own content. Participate in events.

This raises your profile, establishing you as an expert and authority. It expands your credibility footprint. When someone searches for something you're brilliant at, your name comes up.

What gets better

When you become known for your brilliance in your field, you are top of mind when your ideal client has a problem you can fix. You don't burn through marketing spend, hoping you'll convert a lead. You have power. It's a conversation – not a pitch.

What gets worse

If you don't do this, you'll be just another one of many. You'll keep fighting for prospects, you'll waste money chasing them and worry about where the next client will come from.

Call to action: tell them what to do – the predefined purpose of the interaction or content

How great are you at communicating your value and authority? If you want free tips and tactics to reach your next level, sign up for my newsletter.

Here's a top-level summary: start with the most interesting distilled point. 'Why should they care?' is your focus. What action do you want them to take? This is your aim.

When you finish, read it back and ask yourself: does it deliver on your 'Aha!'? Next-level mastery is when you embed hooks throughout the script, keeping your ideal stakeholder engaged and positioning yourself as their solution. Attention is fleeting. Interest lasts. Have something to say. Say it well. Say it often.

Elevate your profile

It's not who you know. It's who knows you.

There are obvious ways to become better known, such as speaking at events, winning awards, and being interviewed. These opportunities require permission.

You need a yes from the person with the power to book you, a yes from those who decide whether your application is worthy.

There is value in each of these, as long as the gate-keeper is credible. Never pay for an interview or any type of accolade – if you're good at what you do and doing interesting things, you will get recognition from the right people. Perhaps not immediately – remember, a 'no' is a 'not yet'.

Here's the thing: you don't need permission to become better known. We live in an age where you can become your own media house, the gateway to valuable information, which leads to growth, income, and your version of success. The only permission you need to get started is your own. I call this raising your profile permission-free.

To increase the probability of you doing this, make it easy. Create content that takes zero extra time and keeps you in your zone of genius. For example, record yourself when on calls with clients – they don't need to know because you won't be using their voice, face, name.

This is ideal because it captures you in your element and in full flow, without the debilitating effects of cerebralising. Use the recordings to establish yourself as your own spokesperson and advocate, and build out a never-ending flow of exceptional unique content via your Infinite Content Machine.

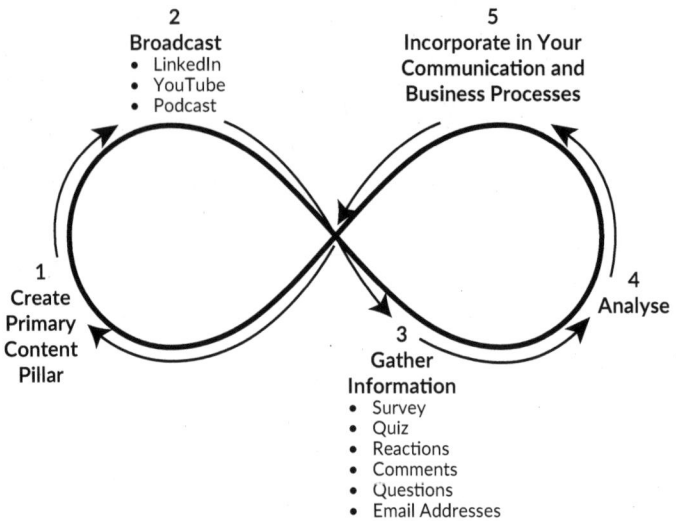

2
Broadcast
- LinkedIn
- YouTube
- Podcast

5
Incorporate in Your Communication and Business Processes

1
Create Primary Content Pillar

4
Analyse

3
Gather Information
- Survey
- Quiz
- Reactions
- Comments
- Questions
- Email Addresses

When creating your Infinite Content Machine, start small and focus on one activity you already do that can be leveraged as your primary communication pillar. Choose the platform where your stakeholder hangs out, get traction and reaction. Use adaptive input-to-output loops, incorporate a mechanism for gathering feedback and data, and critically, leverage this to own direct access to your stakeholders. In today's world, this means gathering email addresses. This is important because platforms come and go, change the way they work and what they allow you to do. Not doing this when I was being beamed into millions of homes every week was a colossal mistake, one that I see many who are riding high on the wave of their success repeating.

Done right, the mechanism to gather stakeholder contact details also documents myths and misconceptions, key words and worries. The insights you gain become deep, valuable, unique data you communicate when you are on the next podcast, share in your posts, and incorporate in your business.

It can be as simple as a LinkedIn post stating 'Our data tell us that the biggest issue facing people in the A field is B'. You're highlighting 'I am', 'I do' and 'I know'.

You are tapping into and borrowing audiences when you guest on others' output, such as a podcast, or when you use LinkedIn, and you are plugging all the resulting insight into your Infinite Content Machine. More of the right type of stakeholder for you fills in your forms, connects directly with you, and consumes your content, ad infinitum.

Note that next-level credibility is not you on you. Appearing as a guest, expert, speaker demonstrates that respected third parties rate you. This is perceived as more valuable than self-promotion, which is why a simple output process, made up of being a regular podcast guest and plugging the resulting content into your Machine, is all that's needed to become known for the right thing by the right people. Doing it this way means your energy can go into what you share and how you share it – the key to your success.

Raise your profile and elevate your authority. Become the gateway to answers and information. It leads you to your next big thing.

Your 24/7 digital agent awaits

Someone somewhere is looking for you right now. They might not be looking for you specifically, but someone in the world has the problem you are brilliant at solving. How can they find you?

I always ask people who I have zero connection with how they know I exist when they get in touch with an opportunity. One answer made me reframe how I see the digital space. The person who got in touch explained that they had used ChatGPT to recommend people with my expertise. My name came up. They narrowed down the search with more niche questions, and my name kept appearing. Then, they tracked me down.

This wasn't because of content I put out recently, but because of a sizeable backlog of credible interactions – speaking engagements, interviews, and articles amassed over many years. This was when ChatGPT only had access to information published up until September 2021; it can now access more recent content. The point I want to get across is that the only way you can be part of the mix is to create your own backlog, starting now.

This interaction made me realise that ChatGPT is my 24/7 agent, as is Google. They work for me for free, whereas my human agent fees start at 20% of my earnings.

Publish now, so you are part of the 'now and next' mix. Get AI and the digital space acting as your agent, and be discovered by people you don't know exist.

Summary

Every interaction is an opportunity – if you nail it.

This chapter offers insights into managing the spotlight during crucial moments with people who influence your success, converting every interaction into active participation. The mantra 'Preparation and practice make persuasive' underscores the essence of the chapter. Strategic preparation and practice pave the way to compelling communication.

The 'Nail It' journey transforms communication hurdles into victories and puts a stop to missed opportunities.

Think. Consolidate the elements of effective communication, focusing on delivering a cohesive, impactful message that's fit for your purpose.

Write. Fine-tune your final message, ensuring it embodies your insights, 'Aha!', and intent. Be ready to make a significant impact, with or without notice.

Speak. Approach every interaction as a chance to practise and perfect your persuasive skills. Engage, inspire, lead to action. Ruffle some feathers!

NINE

T – Transcend Through Action

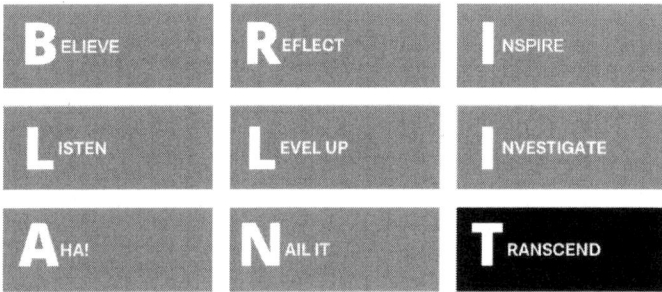

BELIEVE	**R**EFLECT	**I**NSPIRE
LISTEN	**L**EVEL UP	**I**NVESTIGATE
AHA!	**N**AIL IT	**T**RANSCEND

Step into what's next. To get there, embody your next-level self; demonstrate that you possess the credibility and ability to be it, and make it easy for your ideal stakeholders to know about you, find you, and connect with you.

Embrace the notion of building a power base within your field – be known, recognised, and in a category of one. There is no competition or convincing at this level, only conversation. You transcend from The BRILLIANT Communicator, to *The* BRILLIANT Communicator – the only person who brings together the combined lived reality and experiences that make you unique.

Three thoughts for this chapter are:

- Define next you.

- Behave as it. Behave = Be + Have.

- Create your category of one.

Brand you

What three words in terms of function and expertise come to mind when people think of you, see you, or see your name in print? What three words do you want them to associate you with? Do the words that people perceive you to be match what you want to be known for and do more of now? Better still, do the words match what you want to be known for and doing next?

In my personal life, I am the go-to person for everything that's missing, even if I never use it. I want to liberate my grey matter from storing this information by default, and release those whose stuff it is from depending on me to find it – this is 'next us'. I need to set systems and processes in place that enable this – including declaring the paradigm shift, ideally in a way that results in buy-in.

Here are client examples of what I mean. Client A wants to be the go-to person for a niche expertise, a higher-level skill, but is held back by requests that she excels at fulfilling but no longer wants to handle. Not being next A costs her opportunity and income – the higher-level specialisation pays more.

Client B, a partner in a consultancy firm where billable hours are crucial, is frequently drawn into providing foundational how-to guidance to colleagues from other teams. With time equating to money, and the livelihoods of his immediate team at stake, his attention is a valuable commodity, and demands on it compromise his and his team's next success.

What people seek you out for, and assume you to be the go-to person for, can hold you back. However, the solution isn't always a hard no to what you want to push away.

Imagine being able to direct people to a video or an e-document that addresses frequent 'not your focus anymore' queries. You're helping without exhausting your time or energy. With a clear path to how you help now and the stamp of brand 'you' on it, you validate your credentials while associating yourself with your next level of expertise or success.

This approach maintains collaborative relationships while establishing boundaries regarding what you no longer do, without requiring any additional time beyond the creation of the video or document. It also demonstrates your track record and credibility to people who might not know who you are when they come across your independent asset shared online – a later section in this chapter has more on asset building. This is an example of how a problem can become a solution that elevates brand you with existing connections, as well as serving as a calling card.

Don't be burdened by others' dependence on your knowledge; leverage it. Don't dismiss what you used to do; incorporate it.

This week, I was on a call with a group of former corporate professionals turned solopreneurs who are struggling to define their new reality, who they serve, and what they want people to associate them with. Their new go-to will benefit from their previous one when they link the two in a way that serves their current ideal client.

What shows up when someone looks you up, and what people think when they see you or your name, are both elements of brand you. It is the blend of what you do, what you did, what you share, and what others share about you. It encompasses what people hear about you and the impressions they form. Their perceptions, along with the three key words they associate with you, influence their next step – whether they approach you and what for.

Utopia is when your name surfaces as the go-to solution for a problem you excel at solving and want to focus on. Building familiarity with your ideal stakeholder so they see you as their salvation is essential.

How can you fast-track familiarity? That's next.

Build with video

As well as providing pathways for people to find you, publishing content is key to building familiarity with you, your way, and how you share what you know to be true. Which is a great thing for a journalist or producer to know too, as I recently remembered the hard way.

Journalists are human, plus they have no-wiggle deadlines, which means that the path of least resistance, one that indicates more guaranteed results, can be mighty appealing. If someone's name is in print, it signals that they are more likely to say yes to an interview request. If someone has shared content or been interviewed in audio or video format, even better. Here's why.

Having recorded interviews with people whose stories I like – people who have never been interviewed before, and frankly are not great communicators – I am feeling the pain of first-time guestitis. I secretly regret interviewing them because I feel obligated to publish the interviews. Had I heard them elsewhere, I probably wouldn't have chosen to record with them. All this to say, if you are serious about being known for your expertise, get on video – both in your permission-free way and by getting past a gatekeeper – and make sure you're brilliant.

Video is the one medium that no one can emulate. The way you come across, explain things, communicate – it's all you. Plus it has the significant benefit of showing potential hosts how you do you, which helps them decide whether you are a good fit for what they're creating. The last thing you want is to go to the trouble of being interviewed, then being dropped. Getting a call from an embarrassed or miffed minister or CEO who was axed after being interviewed – because they didn't deliver what was needed – was definitely not my favourite thing.

Being on video has another benefit: it provides you with a lot of content for the effort. The soundtrack is numerous audiograms, stills are your images, the transcription is a blog and multiple posts, the recording can become many shorter ones.

What increases the chance of being interviewed? Being interviewed. What increases the chance of being invited back? Being brilliant at it. What's the ultimate way to build familiarity with brand you? Video. What multiplies your online presence with the least effort? Stripping video components.

Build with video. Do it now.

Fast-track your hours online in a flash, and build familiarity with unique you in a dash.

Influence not influencer

You influence when you change the way someone thinks; when you open up a new way of being, doing, solving for them. You have influence when you affect what your stakeholder does next – buy your product, hire you, invest in your company. You become a Person of Influence when you are a trusted, valuable resource and reference, and sought out as the solution.

It's not about fame and followers; it's about being famous where it counts – known and sought after within your field, by your ideal stakeholders.

Influence is the power to direct behaviour.

A fundamental component of influence is crafting strategic assets that amplify brand you. Think of them as resources and products that are of service to the person you want a yes from, cementing your status as the authority and amplifying your position as their solution.

You can add to your brand-you portfolio at warp speed by capitalising on transient interactions and reframing what you deliver as products that last. For example, when you're speaking at an event or hosting a Q&A session with clients, team members, a community – if it's not recorded, only the people in situ will ever know what transpired. If it is captured, it lives on. Record interactions, document findings and insights, repurpose, re-use, and amp up your asset-building process. The higher the bar of entry, the more you cultivate credibility and authority, because fewer people do things that require significant or sustained effort.

Prioritise one-and-done assets, ideally evergreen content where you create the resource once, and it works for you 24/7, potentially for years. Examples include a video series, writing a book or publishing a white paper – each of which also establishes you as a thought leader. Alternatively, it can be ongoing output such as regular LinkedIn or YouTube lives – high-value, high-bar-of-entry assets that contribute to the compounding growth of brand you when you consistently commit.

It's not only about output; it's what you put out too. The gold is your data, existing information in your system, what this signals to your gut, and how it forms your opinion.

People tend to dismiss their most valuable asset – what they know and have access to by virtue of what they do. Mine your current ecosystem for information that can be used to create thought leadership pieces. Information and insight that is unique to you. Frame it in a way that gets client and stakeholder interest and coverage. Point to your call to action at the end of it.

The data you gather via your Infinite Content Machine are particularly valuable as they set you up as a source of credible statistics and trends. Use this to bolster your authority. It could be by way of putting out an industry alert or round table where you can assert, 'Our industry thinks A; experts in our sector want B,' stating clearly that you are extrapolating from your data.

Accessing credible up-to-date information was a huge problem when I covered the region that is Iran to Morocco, Turkey to Sudan. It was scant at best, often not verifiable, and real-time data were a rarity. Guests didn't realise that their experiences and lived realities were invaluable to us, resulting in many hours spent attempting to extract answers that stemmed from their intuition, conclusions, insights, and perspectives, not what was in the press releases put out.

You have the ingredients to be a thought leadership powerhouse. Be it. Max out what you extrapolate from data and touchpoints. Maximise the influence you have as a result.

Power

Feeling powerful makes you powerful. Here's how.

A sense of power translates to better executive function in terms of how your brain works.[20] It increases optimism, creativity, and the ability to self-regulate, which means feeling better overall. Who doesn't want this?

You give off and therefore have a sense of power when you are your 3C self. This means you're noticed and remembered by the right people for you for the right reasons.

I introduced Xavier Sala-i-Martin, one of the world's leading economists and professor of economics at Columbia University, at a conference. It was our first interaction. Xavier couldn't find me when the event ended, so he emailed me. His lovely note highlights the power of listening, being heard, and elevating interactions – also known as being The BRILLIANT Communicator.

> 'I wanted to tell you that you were the most impressive presenter I have ever encountered (and, trust me, I encounter dozens of them every year in every country

in the world). Normally, presenters give well-crafted introductions of the speakers. They research their subjects and so on and so forth, *but they don't listen!* You, on the other hand, paid attention to what was said, commented intelligently on the contributions, related the main ideas of two or more different speakers. In sum, you did an extraordinary job. I am glad that I have the opportunity to tell you.'

It's usually members of an audience who come up to me with similar sentiments. Getting this email from a speaker made me realise how Xavier is an exception on many fronts. Apart from his track record, he is a rare breed of speaker who wants to tune into what others are thinking. He stuck around, getting a feel for the room, discovering presenters' takes on issues – little wonder he is *The* BRILLIANT Communicator in his field.

Many speakers deliver and depart, which can leave an audience with a disjointed feeling – ideas that are repeated, important gaps that remain, a sense that they are not heard, seen or valued beyond filling seats. You create powerful connections when you genuinely seek to discover what your stakeholder wants and needs, their 4Ps, and their biggest aspiration. Sometimes this results in connecting with a person in a position of power – but that's not my point. What's more important is this: the type of connection you curate is powerful, and the right person for you engages – they take the next step.

Some perceive power as a dirty word. It's not. It is what makes things happen. Harness it to get your want. The most direct way to increase your power is to increase your influence and reputation.

Influence plus reputation equals increased power.

The more people know your capabilities and respect – or at least value – what you know and do, the more power you will have. This is important because you achieve what you want and need through people, the stakeholders in your ecosystem. To get them to do your bidding, you can influence, force, or beg.

Influence is much more effective than forcing, and more palatable than pleading. Power is the ability to influence people to take the next step, where they deliver on what you want and need willingly.

A sense of power affects how you are on the inside and how you show up. It attracts people who are powerful too. What makes you feel powerful?

I'm a helicopter

While I was with BBC World, I interviewed Saudi Prince Al Waleed bin Talal when he was one of the richest men in the world. I asked him how he managed the sixty-four companies he was running at the time. Here is the essence of his reply:

'I visualise myself as being in a helicopter, not an aeroplane, because a helicopter can land anywhere, fix things and leave. With aeroplanes, you have to land on the runway, go through customs, get into a car and travel, often getting to where you need to be too late. In a helicopter is how I visualise myself really.

'We have a lot of things we're working on simultaneously. Sure, I'm hands on, but I delegate a lot of power to the people working with me. I trust them. I'm sure they make errors. I make errors. I make mistakes. I have to learn from them.'

My question was standard; the answer isn't.

Most people give textbook responses to similar questions – elements of which bin Talal shared in the second half of his answer. However, he didn't lead with this; he first established his way of doing what he does in his unique way.

A few days after the interview aired, I walked into a World Economic Forum meeting. The Arab world's movers and shakers kept coming up to me and saying, 'I'm a helicopter.' It's the one thought that stuck from the half-hour programme and is all that needed to – because it tells you everything about how bin

Talal thinks, behaves, goes about his business. You get a sense of him. It's a phrase that *is* him. People walking around a conference centre saying it, and knowing exactly who and what it referred to... now, that's power.

Al Waleed bin Talal is in his own category of one. You can be too. Cultivating it includes leaning into your unfair advantages. You have unfair advantages – they're likely things you take for granted, or dismiss. They are often the coming together of the unique path that your life and career have taken. What are they? Define them. Did you merge more than one career or expertise over your lifetime? Have you done something considered extraordinary?

Leaning into your unfair advantages sets you apart by default. Incorporating learnings and insight as a result of them – where relevant – into what you broadcast cements your category of one by definition.

When your best stakeholder knows your unique ingredients, you become the only choice. You transcend from a BRILLIANT Communicator to *The* BRILLIANT Communicator in your field. *The* solution. *The* one. You are chased and chosen.

There is no fixed end point to this; it's an ongoing journey of cultivating your chosen status within your category of one. What evolves includes your signature style.

You are now familiar with how I share information. You have a feel for my way or style of communicating – it reveals how I think. I like to distil, identify three words that summarise what's being discussed, and use short sentences (which I have had to fight against when writing this book). Breaking things down and building them up again with a reason for you to care is my distinctive tone. My wish for you is to discover yours.

Determining your style comes not from forcing it, but liberating it – out of you, into the world. First you must reveal it to yourself.

Lean on The BRILLIANT Communicator's building blocks, and populate them with what makes you, you. You know the rules. Break them. Create your own way, style, communication signature. No one's clone, simply your 3C self.

The 3Cs now point to one: conviction.

Have the conviction to stand by what you know to be true. The conviction to believe in yourself and what you want next. The conviction to go out there and be your unapologetically unique brilliant self.

Summary

Be your own agent and spokesperson. Be your biggest advocate!

None of this happens without you applying what you've learned and said 'Aha!' about, and pursuing what you want for yourself. To realise what's possible, embark on your perpetual phases of begin, get better, get BRILLIANT. Frame the process as a venture into adventure – because that's what life is: an adventure of decisions and discovery. Lean into your unfair advantage and become *The* BRILLIANT Communicator in your field – the only option in your unique category of one. The pain of chasing is then supplanted with the pleasure of being chosen.

We now have our common lexicon and language – you know exactly what I mean when you see the 3Cs or the 4Ps. We are in tune and in flow. You will arrive at your own terminology and vocabulary in due course – which serves to differentiate you, plus bind your stakeholders and community together, as well as to you. I like to think of it as 'the language of you'.

Think. Reflect on how you can become *The* BRILLIANT Communicator in your field, transcending to a category of one.

Write. Outline a plan that addresses your wants, needs, and the steps to achieve them.

Speak. Take action and experience real transformation in your power base, your influence, and your reputation and reach within your field. Enjoy the resulting change in yourself and life.

Conclusion

Who gets the money? Who has impact and influence? Who builds their best life? Who changes the world?

The BRILLIANT Communicator.

This isn't only about money – although money means choice, and you can always give it away if you don't want it. It's about getting what you *really* want out of life.

My biggest message to you is this: we're all going to die, so how do you want to live? It's time to show up for yourself, and for what you believe.

You now know how to communicate with impact and influence, and why it's important you do this. Start doing it – start now. Embed it as a way of thinking and being, and get it working for you. Enjoy what you are worth, stand up for yourself and those you care about, show up as your brilliant self.

A dear friend passed away a few days before I wrote this – his biggest wish was to create videos to share what he knew to be true. Clever, witty, and brave (he survived most of his lungs being blown out by a bomb), he specialised in fraud – I called him the money detective. At one point, he discovered he was unintentionally recovering money for the mafia. My friend fancied himself a bit of a thespian, talked incessantly about recording videos for… a year? More?

The loop he got stuck in was planning to do it and what to wear (he settled on a black T having seen so many others adopt it). His focus on the superficial was a distraction, a subconscious delay tactic. It was safe to talk about it, scary to do it.

I believe it was the 'start' grip of terror that held him back, along with a smidge of 'what will people think?' and liberal lashings of 'what if I am rubbish?' As a consequence, we will never benefit from his vast vault of experience and knowledge – delivered with his acerbic wit by way of his astute mind – because he couldn't get out of his own way.

Hit record. Start. Be. Do. Share.
Get out of your own way.

I hope you will take this as a loving kick up the behind so you implement The BRILLIANT Communicator process and step into your next success. Be your biggest advocate and spokesperson, permission-free, and build your best life.

Sounds cheesy, fantastical, not achievable perhaps. It can be your reality. You need to want it. You need to take action.

Know + Want + Do
× BRILLIANT Communicator
= Your (version of) Success

However, that's not enough. Success isn't the big 'I made it!'; it's that, plus being able to show up, and keep showing up for it. It's building a life that doesn't break you, and that you don't need a break from.

A bit more about me: I have always worked for myself, bar a handful of years when I first started out. I thought I had hit the winning formula – no one was my boss. I was flying around the world – rubbing shoulders with the movers and shakers of industry and government. Living the dream, right?

Wrong.

I was not in control of my time. I was not in control of where I worked from. Chairing and speaking at events, training people at the top of their game, interviewing and filming – it was all person-facing. My success depended on me being on-location.

Yes, I was known and chosen, but I lost out. I didn't drill down to a core go-to that I wanted – I was responding to what others wanted from me. I didn't own direct access to people I wanted in my circle, people who wanted more from me.

This is why Build – Part One – includes figuring out what you want for yourself, now and later. Knowing it directs your next move.

I now define success as doing what I want, when I want, where I want. It sounds childish – it's the most grown up I have ever been, because it pivots on me taking responsibility for me, for what keeps me sane, solvent, sustaining my version of success.

Ambition + Ability + Sanity = Sustainable Success

You can achieve sustainable success if you define, and plan, and have a tremendous bias for the right action. What you know – right now – is your ticket to building a life that sustains and nourishes you, as long as you are known for it by the right people.

I have never applied for an opportunity – I have worked with countless multinationals, global organisations, governments and quasi-government institutions by invitation because a decision maker knew me, or knew about me, and got in touch. I want this for you. For you to be chosen, sought after, top of mind, an opportunity magnet. Making it your reality is not magic – it takes work, commitment, and getting uncomfortable, but when it happens, it's magic.

Own your life. Take ownership of your brilliance and knowledge. Consider it a business – the business of you – whether you work for yourself or not. Being known for your expertise, elevating your profile, owning assets that amplify you – all of this means you lean into your earning potential and your life's potential.

What you know equals
opportunity and income – only
if you're known for it.

At the core of all of this is: be better at sharing what you want, need, and do; what you are the go-to person for, who you serve, and why they should choose you. Doing it well is the foundation of everything good to come.

I hope you have benefited from and enjoyed reading this book. It has been a joy to create. If you know someone who could do with reading it, please share it with them (or buy it for them).

Are you ready to find out how you measure up as a BRILLIANT Communicator? Take the self-assessment at: www.thebrilliantcommunicator.com/self-assessment and receive your free personalised report.

Your report will deliver actionable tactics and tips to help you communicate with greater impact and influence. Let's begin your journey to becoming The BRILLIANT Communicator you're meant to be today!

I hope you are inspired to take the next step on your path to being The BRILLIANT Communicator in your field, and thereafter becoming *The* BRILLIANT Communicator – creating your category of one. Here's to transcending from chase to chosen. Here's to your best life. Here's to what's next.

Here's to BRILLIANT you.

Notes

1   Y Liu, EA Piazza, E Simony, PA Shewokis,
    B Onaral, U Hasson, H Ayaz, 'Measuring
    speaker–listener neural coupling with functional
    near infrared spectroscopy', *Scientific Reports*
    (27 February 2017), www.nature.com / articles /
    srep43293, accessed 8 September 2024
2   A Mehrabian, M Wiener, 'Decoding of
    inconsistent communications', *Journal of
    Personality and Social Psychology*, 6 / 1 (1967)
    109–114, https: / / psycnet.apa.org / record / 1967-
    08861-001?doi=1, accessed 8 September
    2024; A Mehrabian, SR Ferris, 'Inference of
    attitudes from nonverbal communication in
    two channels', *Journal of Consulting Psychology*,
    31 / 3 (1967) 248–252, https: / / doi.org / 10.1037 /
    h0024648, accessed 8 September 2024

3   M Schwantes, 'Warren Buffett says there's one skill that will raise your value by an astounding fifty percent, *Inc.* (2 June 2022), www.inc.com/marcel-schwantes/warren-buffett-says-theres-1-skill-that-will-raise-your-value-by-an-astounding-50-percent.html, accessed 8 September 2024

4   DI Tamir, JP Mitchell, 'Disclosing information about the self is intrinsically rewarding', *PNAS*, 109/21 (2012), 8038–8043, www.pnas.org/doi/full/10.1073/pnas.1202129109, accessed 22 July 2024

5   LA Ovington, AJ Saliba, CC Moran, J Goldring, JB MacDonald, 'Do people really have insights in the shower? The when, where and who of the Aha! moment', *Journal of Creative Behavior* (28 November 2015), https://doi.org/10.1002/jocb.126, accessed 8 September 2024; ZC Irving, C McGrath, L Flynn, A Glasser, C Mills, 'The shower effect: Mind wandering facilitates creative incubation during moderately engaging activities', *Psychology of Aesthetics, Creativity, and the Arts* (advance online publication, 2022), https://doi.org/10.1037/aca0000516, accessed 8 September 2024

6   K Umejima, T Ibaraki, T Yamazaki, KL Sakai, 'Paper notebooks vs mobile devices: Brain activation differences during memory retrieval', *Frontiers in Behavioral Neuroscience*, 15 (2021), www.ncbi.nlm.nih.gov/pmc/articles/PMC8017158, accessed 22 July 2024

7   FR Van der Weel, ALH Van der Meer, 'Handwriting but not typewriting leads to widespread brain connectivity: A high-density EEG study with implications for the classroom', *Frontiers in Psychology*, 14 (2024), https://doi.org/10.3389/fpsyg.2023.1219945, accessed 22 July 2024; PA Mueller, DM Oppenheimer, 'The pen is mightier than the keyboard: Advantages of longhand over laptop note taking', *Psychological Science*, 25/6 (2014), 1159–1168, https://doi.org/10.1177/0956797614524581, accessed 22 July 2024

8   NA Coles, DS March, F Marmolejo-Ramos, et al, 'A multi-lab test of the facial feedback hypothesis by the Many Smiles Collaboration', *Nature Human Behaviour*, 6 (2022), 1731–1742, https://doi.org/10.1038/s41562-022-01458-9, accessed 22 July 2024

9   S Söderkvist, K Ohlén and U Dimberg, 'How the experience of emotion is modulated by facial feedback', *Journal of Nonverbal Behavior*, 42 (2017), 129–151, https://link.springer.com/article/10.1007/s10919-017-0264-1, accessed 22 July 2024

10 A Cuddy, 'Your body language may shape who you are' (TEDGlobal, 2012), www.ted.com/talks/amy_cuddy_your_body_language_may_shape_who_you_are?language=en, accessed 22 July 2024

11 M Kim, 'Think leader, think deep voice? CEO voice pitch and gender', *Academy of Management*

Proceedings, 1 (2022), https://journals.aom.org/
doi/abs/10.5465/AMBPP.2022.17778abstract,
accessed 22 July 2024; M Burkley, 'Why deep-
voiced politicians get more votes: The science
of pitch-perfect politics', *Psychology Today* (11
September 2018), www.psychologytoday.com/
gb/blog/the-social-thinker/201809/why-deep-
voiced-politicians-get-more-votes, accessed
22 July 2024; CA Klofstad, RC Anderson, S
Nowicki, 'Perceptions of competence, strength,
and age influence voters to select leaders
with lower-pitched voices', *PLoS ONE* 10/8
(2015), https://journals.plos.org/plosone/
article?id=10.1371/journal.pone.0133779,
accessed 22 July 2024

12 WJ Mayew, CA Parsons, M Venkatachalam,
'Voice pitch and the labor market success of
male chief executive officers', *Evolution and
Human Behavior*, 34/4 (2013), 243–248, www.
sciencedirect.com/science/article/abs/pii/
S1090513813000238, accessed 22 July 2024

13 K Reich, 'Walter E Deimer; inventor of bubble
gum', *Los Angeles Times* (13 January 1998), www.
latimes.com/archives/la-xpm-1998-jan-13-mn-
7854-story.html, accessed 25 July 2024

14 *Accounting Today*, '10 Celebrity almost CPAs' (26
November 2013), www.accountingtoday.com/
slideshow/10-celebrity-almost-cpas, accessed 25
July 2024

15 Ziacom Medical, 'The Egyptian Hesy-Ra was
the first dentist to treat the tooth decay of the

pharaohs' (no date), https://ziacom.com/en/
hesy-ra-the-first-dentist-in-history, accessed 25
July 2024

16 *British Dental Journal*, 'More than half of dentists
say stress is affecting their practice', *BDJ* , 226/7
(2019), www.nature.com/articles/sj.bdj.2019.18,
accessed 22 July 2024

17 BJ Miller, 'Scientists are making cochineal, a red
dye from bugs, in the lab', *Smithsonian Magazine*,
(29 March 2022), www.smithsonianmag.com/
innovation/scientists-are-making-cochineal-
a-red-dye-from-bugs-in-the-lab-180979828,
accessed 22 July 2024

18 M Gibson, 'Cheese is the most stolen food
on Earth', *Time* (21 October 2011), https://
newsfeed.time.com/2011/10/21/cheese-is-the-
most-stolen-food-on-earth, accessed 22 July 2024

19 C Cassella, 'Cheese makes you happy and could
boost healthy aging, study suggests', *Science
Alert* (20 June 2024), www.sciencealert.com/
cheese-makes-you-happy-and-could-boost-
healthy-aging-study-suggests, accessed 14
October 2024

20 Y Yin, PK Smith, 'Power and cognitive
functioning', *Current Opinion in Psychology*, 33
(2020), 95–99, www.sciencedirect.com/science/
article/abs/pii/S2352250X19301009, accessed 22
July 2024

Acknowledgements

I t is done. A big, heartfelt thank you to everyone who helped bring this book to life. I am deeply honoured by the generous contributions of those who took the time to read the draft and offer their input.

I couldn't have hoped for a better foreword, penned by powerhouse and entrepreneur Fadi Ghandour. In just a few sentences he managed to sum up the book, entice the right reader to dive in, and bring to life the exact reasons I wrote it. Fadi's wisdom, drawn from a lifetime of leadership and much experience, brings added depth to this work, and sets it up perfectly. Fadi, thank you.

Thank you, too, to the people mentioned in the book, along with those who entrusted me with the opportunity to be part of their journey. You have provided insight and joy – and have helped shape what I share.

To my beta readers and those who provided statements of praise – Andrea Sparke, Ashraf Shakah, Ausar Stewart, David Savage, Lady Eve Laws, Mark Beer OBE, Michaella Brown, Pedro Moss, HRH Princess Rym Ali, and Tom Kenyon-Slaney – your keen contributions have been instrumental in refining the content and underscoring the significance and value of this book.

A special thanks to Joe Gregory, my publisher, who started this journey with me and ensured I got through it, as well as the magnificent team at Rethink Press. Special mention to Alison, Anke, and Kathleen.

To the brave individuals I've encountered who are inventing their version of success, I love what you're doing, keep going.

And to my wonderful son and my dog, I am eternally indebted. Both have been exceptionally patient and are my biggest champions and supporters.

Thank you, one and all. It has been a blast.

The Author

With decades of experience on global TV – her last stint was twelve years on BBC World – and stages worldwide, along with teaching the C-Suite how to become brilliant communicators, Nima Abu Wardeh combines first-hand experience with reality-based know-how. Her practical, no-BS approach empowers clients to transform the way they think, write, and speak, enabling them to establish themselves as credible experts in their field, and go on to become a person of influence, in their category of one.

She has worked with, developed, booked, inter-viewed, and shared platforms alongside the world's most influential people. Nima's lived experience, along with her MSc in Medical Engineering – undertaken because she is interested in how the brain operates and the workings of the human condition – places her in a category of one. She leverages this knowledge to develop practical, proven systems that take people from chasing opportunities to being chosen.

Discover how you measure up as The BRILLIANT Communicator. Take the self-assessment and get actionable tips to communicate with impact and influence at:

🌐 www.thebrilliantcommunicator.com